YOUR recipe could appear in our next cookbook!

Share your tried & true family favorites with us instantly at
www.gooseberrypatch.com
If you'd rather jot 'em down by hand, just mail this form to...
Gooseberry Patch • Cookbooks – Call for Recipes
PO Box 812 • Columbus, OH 43216-0812

If your recipe is selected for a book, you'll receive a FREE copy!

Please share only your original recipes or those that you have made your own over the years.

Recipe Name:

Number of Servings:

Any fond memories about this recipe? Special touches you like to add
or handy shortcuts?

Ingredients (include specific measurements):

T0015690

Instructions (continue on back if needed):

Special Code: **cookbookspage**

Over ➤

Extra space for recipe if needed:

Tell us about yourself...

Your complete contact information is needed so that we can send you your FREE cookbook, if your recipe is published. Phone numbers and email addresses are kept private and will only be used if we have questions about your recipe.

Name:

Address:

City: State: Zip:

Email:

Daytime Phone:

Thank you! Vickie & Jo Ann

Gooseberry Patch

An imprint of Globe Pequot
64 South Main Street
Essex, CT 06426

www.gooseberrypatch.com

1•800•854•6673

Do you have a tried & true recipe...

tip, craft or memory that you'd like to see featured in
a **Gooseberry Patch** cookbook? Visit our website at
www.gooseberrypatch.com, register and follow the
easy steps to submit your favorite family recipe.
Or send them to us at:

Gooseberry Patch
PO Box 812
Columbus, OH 43216-0812

Don't forget to include the number of servings your recipe makes,
plus your name, address, phone number and email address. If we
select your recipe, your name will appear right along with it...
and you'll receive a **FREE** copy of the book!

◆ Contents ◆

❖ Dedication ❖

To everyone who wants to slow
down and enjoy a good,
home-cooked meal!

❖ Appreciation ❖

Thanks to all our friends who
shared their favorite
slow-cooker recipes!

MADE
with
LOVE

LOW ▲   ▲ HIGH

Family Favorites

Mains and one-pot meals

Tammy's Italian Chicken

Julie Klum
Lake Oswego, OR

Everyone loves this quick & easy dish! My son gets a thumbs-up from the other firefighters on his crew when it's his turn to cook, and my sister-in-law got rave reviews when she served it to her son's high school football team.

2-1/2 lbs. frozen chicken breasts
1-1/2 oz. pkg. spaghetti
    sauce mix
14-1/2 oz. can diced tomatoes

8-oz. can tomato sauce
cooked penne pasta
Garnish: grated Parmesan
    cheese

Arrange frozen chicken in a slow cooker. Sprinkle with sauce mix; add tomatoes and tomato sauce. Cover and cook on low setting for 7 to 8 hours, or on high setting for 3-1/2 to 4-1/2 hours. Serve over penne pasta, sprinkled with Parmesan cheese. Makes 4 to 6 servings.

Early American homes always had a kettle of savory stew bubbling at the back of the fireplace. With a slow cooker on your kitchen counter, you can cook up the same delicious slow-simmered flavor!

Sunshine Chicken

Fawn McKenzie
Wenatchee, WA

This sauce is terrific over ribs and chops too!

6 boneless, skinless chicken
   breasts
1/4 c. molasses
2 T. cider vinegar

2 T. Worcestershire sauce
2 T. orange juice
2 t. Dijon mustard
1/8 to 1/4 t. hot pepper sauce

Arrange chicken in a slow cooker; set aside. Combine remaining ingredients and brush over chicken. Cover and cook on low setting for 7 to 9 hours, or on high setting for 3 to 4 hours. Serves 6.

Try not to peek! It's hard, when the food just smells so good, but total cooking time increases by 15 to 20 minutes every time a slow cooker's lid is lifted.

Honey-Mustard Short Ribs

David Wink
Marion, Ohio

If your grocer carries boneless short ribs, cooking time can be reduced by about an hour.

3 to 4 lbs. bone-in beef
   short ribs
salt and pepper to taste
1 c. hickory smoke-flavored
   barbecue sauce

3 T. honey
1 T. Dijon mustard
3 cloves garlic, minced
2 T. cornstarch
2 T. cold water

Sprinkle ribs with salt and pepper; place in a slow cooker and set aside. Combine barbecue sauce, honey, mustard, garlic and additional salt and pepper, if desired; pour over ribs. Cover and cook on low setting for 6 to 7 hours. During the last 30 minutes of cooking, whisk cornstarch into water; add to slow cooker, stirring until thickened. Serves 4.

Thaw frozen roasts before slow cooking, if possible. Otherwise, cook on high for the first hour, then reduce to low and cook as usual...ingredients will rise quickly to a safe temperature.

Mustard Pork Chops & Taters

*Amy Butcher
Columbus, GA*

So yummy...you won't believe it's so easy to fix!

2 T. oil
6 to 8 pork loin chops
10-3/4 oz. can cream of
    mushroom soup
1/4 c. chicken broth
1/4 c. country Dijon mustard

1 clove garlic, minced
1/2 t. dried thyme
1/4 t. pepper
5 potatoes, peeled and thinly
    sliced
1 onion, sliced

Heat oil in large skillet over medium heat. Add pork chops and brown on both sides; drain. Combine soup, chicken broth, mustard, garlic, thyme and pepper in a slow cooker. Add potatoes and onion, stirring to coat. Arrange pork chops on top of potatoes. Cover and cook on low setting for 8 to 10 hours, or on high setting for 4 to 5 hours. Makes 6 to 8 servings.

Little or no added liquid is needed in slow cooking...just add what's called for. There's no evaporation so you'll actually end up with more liquid than you started with!

Mom's Cabbage Rolls

Dixie Dill
Elkland, MO

*My mom gave me this recipe when I was a frazzled newlywed. It's
simple and delicious, especially good on a cold winter day.*

1-1/2 lbs. ground beef
1/2 c. instant rice, uncooked
1 egg
1 t. garlic powder

1/2 t. salt
1/2 t. pepper
1 onion, diced
12 to 14 cabbage leaves

Mix together all ingredients except cabbage leaves; set aside. Drop
cabbage leaves into boiling water for 3 to 4 minutes, until pliable;
drain. Place 1/4 cup ground beef mixture in the center of each leaf.
Fold in sides, then roll to make a neat sausage-shaped package;
set aside. Pour half the sauce into a slow cooker; add cabbage rolls.
Pour remaining sauce over rolls. Cover and cook on high setting for
5 to 6 hours. Serves 4 to 6.

Sauce:

2 8-oz. cans tomato sauce
juice of 2 lemons

3 T. all-purpose flour
1/2 c. sugar

Combine all ingredients in a bowl; mix well.

Slow cookers are so handy, you may want more than one!
A 5-1/2 or 6-quart model is just right for families and
potlucks...a smaller 3-quart one will cook for 2 or can
be used for dips and sauces.

Spaghetti Sauce for a Crowd
Kathie Lorenzini
Ignacio, CO

This is my daughter Kerrie's recipe...we think it's the best!

28-oz. can crushed tomatoes
15-oz. can tomato sauce
12-oz. can tomato paste
1/2 c. onion, chopped
2 cloves garlic, minced
3 T. sugar
1 t. dried basil

1 t. dried oregano
1/2 t. salt
20-oz. pkg. Italian sausage
   links, browned, drained
   and sliced
2 16-oz. pkgs. spaghetti,
   cooked

Stir together all ingredients except sausages and spaghetti in a slow cooker. Add sausages; cover and cook on low for 8 hours. Serve sauce over cooked spaghetti. Serves 12 to 14.

Slow-cooked spaghetti sauce adds homemade flavor to oh-so many meals. Bake it with penne pasta and mushrooms, spoon it over a meatloaf or just toss with spaghetti...you'll want to make plenty to freeze for later!

Aloha Chicken

Yvonne Van Brimmer
Apple Valley, CA

I like to serve this over steamed rice, sprinkled with fresh coconut flakes for an extra taste of the tropics.

4 lbs. boneless, skinless chicken
20-oz. can pineapple chunks
11-oz. can mandarin oranges,
   drained
1 green or red pepper, chopped

1/4 c. onion, chopped
1 clove garlic, minced
1 T. soy sauce
1 t. fresh ginger, peeled and
   grated

Arrange chicken in a slow cooker; set aside. Combine remaining ingredients; pour over chicken. Cover and cook on low setting for 8 to 10 hours. Serves 8 to 10.

Spray the crock with non-stick vegetable spray before adding ingredients...clean-up's a snap!

Grandma's Garlic Chicken

Darcy Geiger
Columbia City, IN

One of my most cherished recipes from my grandmother.

6 to 8 boneless, skinless
   chicken breasts
4 c. water
16-oz. bottle Italian salad
   dressing
1/4 c. onion, diced

1/4 c. soy sauce
2 T. oil
2 T. lemon juice
2 T. dried parsley
1 T. garlic, minced

Combine all ingredients in a large plastic zipping bag; refrigerate overnight. Transfer chicken mixture to a slow cooker. Cover and cook on low setting for 4 hours. Increase to high setting and cook for an additional 2 hours, or until chicken juices run clear. Serves 4 to 6.

So just how hot does a slow cooker get? On the low setting, 200 degrees...on high, 300 degrees.

Spanish Rice

Gloria Bills
Plymouth, MI

An old standby...kids love it.

2 lbs. ground beef, browned
    and drained
2 onions, chopped
2 green peppers, chopped
28-oz. can diced tomatoes
8-oz. can tomato sauce

1 c. long-cooking rice, uncooked
1 c. water
2-1/2 t. chili powder
2-1/2 t. salt
2 t. Worcestershire sauce

Combine all ingredients in a slow cooker; stir thoroughly. Cover and cook on low setting for 6 to 8 hours, or on high setting for 3 to 4 hours. Serves 6.

Use long-cooking rice for all-day cooking...it won't turn mushy like instant rice. Or cook rice separately and stir in when food is nearly done cooking.

Santa Fe Turkey Stew

Michele Dochat
Lilitz, PA

One of my all-time favorites! Serve in big bowls with shredded cheese, sour cream and tortilla chips for scooping...you'll love it too! If your slow cooker is small, it's easy to halve this recipe.

2 16-oz. cans pinto beans
2 16-oz. cans navy beans
2 16-oz. cans black beans
2 16-oz. cans kidney beans
3 lbs. cooked turkey, cubed
2 to 3 6-oz. pkgs. frozen
    shoepeg corn
28-oz. can diced tomatoes

1 c. onion, diced
4 to 5 stalks celery, diced
3 1-oz. pkgs. ranch salad
    dressing mix
1-1/4 oz. pkg. taco seasoning
    mix
salt and pepper to taste
3 14-1/2 oz. cans chicken broth

Drain and rinse all beans; combine with remaining ingredients except broth in a 6-1/2 quart slow cooker. Add enough broth to cover ingredients. Cover and cook on low setting for 8 to 10 hours, or on high setting for 4 hours. Serves 10 to 12.

Cook once, eat twice! Save half the dish in a freezer-safe container and freeze for up to 3 months. Thaw overnight in the fridge...reheat in a saucepan or in the microwave. It's like a free dinner!

French Onion Beef

Dawn Dodge
Roscommon, MI

*Add a tossed green salad and a basket of bakery rolls
for a complete meal.*

1-1/4 lbs. boneless beef
  round steak, cut into 6 pieces
8-oz. pkg. sliced mushrooms
1 c. onion, sliced and separated
  into rings
10-3/4 oz. can French
  onion soup

6-1/4 oz. pkg. herb-flavored
  stuffing mix
1/4 c. butter, melted
8-oz. pkg. shredded mozzarella
  cheese

Layer half of beef, mushrooms and onion in a slow cooker; repeat
layers. Pour soup over top; cover and cook on low setting for 8 to
10 hours. Shortly before serving, toss stuffing mix with its seasoning
packet, melted butter and 1/2 cup liquid from slow cooker. Spread
stuffing mixture on top of beef. Increase to high setting; cover and
cook for 10 minutes, or until stuffing is fluffy. Sprinkle with cheese;
cover and heat until cheese is melted. Serves 4 to 6.

To brown or not to brown? If you prefer, toss meat with
all-purpose flour and brown in a skillet with a little oil.
It's not really necessary though! The exception is
ground meat...browning eliminates excess grease.

◈ Family Favorites ◈
Mains and one-pot meals

Hearty Beef Stew

Maxie Martin
Granbury, TX

This is so easy to get ready the night before! I do all the peeling and chopping, cover the potatoes with water so they won't turn brown in the fridge...then just toss it all together in the morning!

6 potatoes, peeled and cubed
6 carrots, peeled and cut into
   3-inch pieces
3 lbs. stew beef, cut into
   1-1/2 inch cubes
1/3 c. soy sauce
1 t. paprika

1 t. salt
1/2 t. pepper
3 T. all-purpose flour
12-oz. pkg. frozen chopped
   onions
10-1/2 oz. can beef broth
8-oz. can tomato sauce

Arrange potatoes in a slow cooker; top with carrots. Add beef; sprinkle with soy sauce, paprika, salt, pepper, flour and onions. Combine broth and tomato sauce; pour over top. Cover and cook for 9 to 10 hours on low setting, or 4-1/2 to 5 hours on high setting. Serves 8 to 10.

Surprisingly, potatoes and carrots can take longer
to cook than meat...put them into the slow cooker first
and they'll cook faster. Cut veggies into equal-size
cubes for even cooking.

17

Autumn Nutmeg Chicken

Marilyn Morel
Keene, NH

This is so creamy and yummy! The nutmeg lends a sweetness that's complemented by the rosemary, sage and thyme.

6 boneless, skinless chicken
   breast halves
1 to 2 T. oil
1 onion, chopped
1/4 c. fresh parsley, minced
2 10-3/4 oz. cans cream of
   mushroom soup

1/2 c. sour cream
1/2 c. milk
1 T. nutmeg
1/4 t. dried rosemary
1/4 t. dried sage
1/4 t. dried thyme
cooked rice

In a skillet over medium heat, brown chicken in oil; reserve drippings. Arrange chicken in a slow cooker; set aside. Sauté onion and parsley in reserved drippings until onion is tender. Add remaining ingredients except rice; mix well and pour over chicken. Cover and cook on low setting for 5 hours, or until juices run clear when chicken is pierced. Serve over cooked rice. Makes 6 servings.

Slow cookers work best when filled 1/2 to 2/3 full
with ingredients.

Country Chicken Dinner

Amanda Lusignolo
Dublin, OH

A one-pot meal just like Mom used to make.

3 c. potatoes, peeled and cubed
3 c. baby carrots
1 onion, coarsely chopped
4 chicken breasts, halved
1 c. water
2 .87-oz. pkgs. chicken
   gravy mix

1 t. seasoned salt
1 t. dried thyme
1/4 t. poultry seasoning
1 c. sour cream

Arrange potatoes, carrots and onion in a slow cooker. Arrange chicken on top, overlapping slightly; set aside. Combine water, gravy mix and seasonings in a small bowl; drizzle over chicken. Cover and cook on low setting for 8 hours, or on high setting for 4 hours. Remove chicken and vegetables to a serving platter. Whisk sour cream into drippings in slow cooker; pour over chicken and vegetables. Serves 4 to 6.

Stir in dairy products like sour cream and half-and-half during the final 15 to 30 minutes...they won't curdle or break down.

Joyce's 12-Layer Grub

Joyce Cecsarini
Lake Stevens, WA

Very hearty...tastes even better the next day!

2 lbs. ground beef
1/2 c. onion, diced
4 stalks celery, diced
salt and pepper to taste
1-1/2 to 2 c. cabbage, shredded
3 to 4 carrots, peeled and diced
15-oz. can peas, drained

14-1/2 oz. can green beans, drained
15-1/4 oz. can corn, drained
3 to 4 potatoes, peeled and diced
14-1/2 oz. can stewed tomatoes
10-1/2 oz. can beef broth

Layer ground beef, onion and celery in a slow cooker, sprinkling each layer generously with salt and pepper. Add remaining ingredients in order given, sprinkling with additional salt and pepper between layers if desired. Cover and cook on low setting for 8 hours, stirring after 4 hours to break up ground beef. Serves 8.

Add a tasty crunchy topping to slow-cooked casseroles...try finely crushed cheese crackers, herbed stuffing mix or even barbecue potato chips!

Slow-Cooker Breakfast Casserole *Felice Jones*
Boise, ID

Why only eat breakfast in the morning? With this super-simple slow-cooker dish, you can come home from work to the warm & filling flavors of breakfast for dinner!

32-oz. pkg. frozen diced
    potatoes
1 lb. bacon, diced and cooked
1 onion, diced
1 green pepper, diced
1/2 c. shredded Monterey Jack
    cheese

1 doz. eggs
1 c. milk
1 t. salt
1 t. pepper

Layer 1/3 each of potatoes, bacon, onion, green pepper and cheese. Repeat layers 2 more times, ending with a layer of cheese. In a bowl, beat together eggs, milk, salt and pepper. Pour over mixture in slow cooker. Cover and cook on low setting for 8 to 9 hours. Serves 8 to 10.

Adapt a favorite family recipe to slow cooking...simple! Cut liquid in half and convert simmering or baking time as follows:

35 to 45 minutes = 6 to 8 hours on low
or 3 to 4 on high
one to 3 hours = 8 to 16 hours on low
or 4 to 6 on high

Crock O' Brats

Naomi Cooper
Delaware, OH

*Serve with hearty rye bread and homestyle applesauce
sprinkled with cinnamon.*

20-oz. pkg. bratwurst
5 potatoes, peeled and cubed
1 tart apple, cored and cubed
1 onion, chopped

1/4 c. brown sugar, packed
1/2 t. salt
27-oz. can sauerkraut, drained

Brown bratwurst in a large skillet over medium heat; reserve
drippings. Slice bratwurst into one-inch pieces; set aside. Combine
remaining ingredients in a slow cooker. Stir in bratwurst slices with
pan drippings. Cover and cook on high setting for 4 to 6 hours, or
until potatoes are tender. Serves 6.

There's usually no need for stirring! A slow cooker
surrounds food with even heat...it won't scorch on
the bottom. If you do stir, be sure to put the lid back
on as quickly as possible.

Pintos & Pork Over Corn Chips
Susan Butters
Bountiful, UT

Feeds a crowd of hungry people...easy!

16-oz. pkg. dried pinto beans
3-lb. pork loin roast
7 c. water
4-oz. can chopped green chiles
1/2 c. onion, chopped
2 cloves garlic, minced
2 T. chili powder

1 T. ground cumin
1 T. salt
1 t. oregano
Garnish: corn chips, sour cream,
  shredded Cheddar cheese,
  chopped tomatoes,
  shredded lettuce

Cover beans with water in a large soup pot; soak overnight. Drain.
Add beans and remaining ingredients except garnish to a slow cooker.
Cover and cook on low setting for 9 hours; remove meat from bones
and return to slow cooker. Cook, uncovered, for 30 minutes until
thickened. Serve over corn chips, garnished as desired. Serves 10.

Make a bridal shower gift extra special...fill up a slow
cooker with seasoning mix packets, herbs & spices.
You can even tuck in a mini cookbook...the new bride
will appreciate your thoughtfulness!

Old-Fashioned Bean Soup

Kathleen Poritz
Burlington, WI

I'm a teacher's aide with outdoor winter recess duty...brrr!
So I freeze any extra bean soup in small containers to take
for lunch. It really warms the body & soul!

16-oz. pkg. dried navy beans
2 qts. water
1 meaty ham bone
1 onion, chopped

1/2 c. celery leaves, chopped
5 whole peppercorns
salt to taste
Optional: bay leaf

Cover beans with water in a large soup pot; soak overnight. Drain.
Combine beans, water and remaining ingredients in a slow cooker.
Cover and cook on low setting for 10 to 12 hours, or on high setting
for 5 to 6 hours. Remove ham bone; dice meat and return to slow
cooker. Discard bay leaf, if using. Makes 8 to 10 servings.

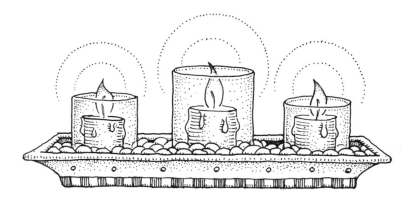

Set lighted votives on a tray filled with dried beans
for a quick & easy centerpiece.

Slow-Cooker Sweet Potato Chili

Cheryl Fernstrom
Exeter, RI

The vegetables cook up nice and bright! A tasty warm-you-up meal on a cold and windy day.

28-oz. can diced tomatoes
16-oz. can black beans, drained and rinsed
16-oz. can kidney beans, drained and rinsed
1 onion, chopped
1 red pepper, chopped
1 green pepper, chopped
3 to 4 stalks celery, chopped

2 sweet potatoes, peeled and cut into 1/2-inch cubes
Optional: 1 lb. ground beef or ground turkey, browned and drained; canned diced jalapeños or hot pepper sauce to taste
8-oz. pkg. shredded Mexican-blend or Cheddar cheese

Combine all ingredients except cheese in a slow cooker; stir to mix. Cover and cook on low setting 8 to 10 hours, or on high setting 4 to 5 hours. Garnish with cheese. Serves 6.

Bake some crisp cornbread sticks to go with chili! Simply stir up a corn muffin mix, pour into a cast iron cornstick pan and bake according to package directions. Yummy!

Burgundy Meatloaf

Vickie

A mixture of ground beef and ground pork can also be used.

2 lbs. ground beef
2 eggs
1 c. soft bread crumbs
1 onion, chopped
1/2 c. Burgundy wine or
    beef broth
1/2 c. fresh parsley, chopped

1 T. fresh basil, chopped
1-1/2 t. salt
1/4 t. pepper
5 slices bacon
1 bay leaf
8-oz. can tomato sauce

Combine ground beef, eggs, crumbs, onion, wine or broth and seasonings in a large bowl; mix well and set aside. Criss-cross 3 bacon slices on a 12-inch square of aluminum foil. Form meat mixture into a 6-inch round loaf on top of bacon. Cut remaining bacon slices in half; arrange on top of meatloaf. Place bay leaf on top. Lift meatloaf by aluminum foil into a slow cooker; cover and cook on high setting for one hour. Reduce to low setting and continue cooking, covered, for an additional 4 hours. Remove meatloaf from slow cooker by lifting foil. Place on a serving platter, discarding foil, bacon and bay leaf. Warm tomato sauce and spoon over sliced meatloaf. Serves 4 to 6.

Tote along a slow-cooker dish to the church supper
or neighborhood block party...plug it back in as soon
as you arrive. The food will be hot and tasty!

◆ Family Favorites ◆
Mains and one-pot meals

Swiss Steak

Jean Carter
Rockledge, FL

I have served this for years to a variety of very picky eaters...they all loved it! Buttery mashed potatoes are delicious alongside.

2 lbs. boneless beef round steak, cut into 6 serving pieces
1.1-oz. pkg. beefy onion soup mix
3 c. onion, sliced
28-oz. can diced tomatoes
3 T. all-purpose flour
1 c. water

Arrange steak in a slow cooker. Sprinkle soup mix over steak; arrange onion slices all around. Top with tomatoes. Cover and cook on low setting for 8 hours, or on high setting for 6 hours. Remove steak and vegetables from slow cooker; set aside. Mix together flour and water; add to slow cooker and stir until thickened. Spoon gravy over steak to serve. Makes 4 to 6 servings.

Add zest to a soup or stew recipe...easy! Just choose a seasoned variety of canned diced tomatoes like Italian or Mexican.

Homestyle Pork Chops

Delina Jenkins
Hamilton, GA

Makes lots of delicious gravy to serve over rice or potatoes.

1/2 c. all-purpose flour
1-1/2 t. dry mustard
1/2 t. salt
1/2 t. garlic powder

6 pork chops
2 T. oil
10-1/2 oz. can chicken broth

Combine flour, mustard, salt and garlic powder in a shallow bowl. Coat pork chops in mixture; set aside any remaining mixture. In a skillet, brown pork chops in oil; drain. Stir together broth and remaining flour mixture in a slow cooker; add pork chops. Cover and cook on high setting for 2-1/2 hours. Makes 6 servings.

Try using cream of chicken, celery or mushroom soup
instead of milk or cream when adapting a recipe
to slow cooking. The soup can cook for a long
time without curdling.

Chicken in the Garden

Linda Karner
Pisgah Forest, NC

We enjoy this served over egg noodles.

2 T. olive oil
2 T. butter
4 boneless, skinless chicken
   breasts
1 onion, sliced
3 carrots, peeled and cut into
   2-inch pieces

10-3/4 oz. can cream of
   chicken soup
1 c. shredded Cheddar cheese
Optional: 1/2 c. sherry or
   Marsala wine
16-oz. pkg. frozen peas

Heat olive oil and butter in a pan until butter is melted. Add chicken breasts; cook until golden and set aside. Place onion slices and carrots in a slow cooker. Arrange chicken breasts on top of carrots; set aside. Mix together soup, cheese and sherry or wine, if using; pour over chicken mixture. Cover and cook on low setting for 6 hours. Add frozen peas; mix well and continue to cook for an additional hour. Serves 4.

Frozen veggies look and taste best when added near the
end of cooking time. Run cold water over them in a
colander to separate them easily.

Corned Beef & Cabbage Soup

Kathy Moser
Allison, PA

Delicious with homemade buns and butter!

12-oz. can corned beef
6 c. water
3 to 4 c. cabbage, cut into
    bite-size pieces

4 to 5 potatoes, peeled and
    cubed
salt and pepper to taste

Combine all ingredients in a slow cooker. Cover and cook on low
setting for 4 to 6 hours, or until potatoes are tender. Serves 4.

Savory Beef Stew

Jennifer Wilson
Saginaw, TX

In a hurry? Just add the beef without browning.

1 t. oil
1 lb. boneless beef round
    steak, cubed
3 potatoes, peeled and cubed
1 c. baby carrots
14-1/2 oz. can beef broth

14-1/2 oz. can stewed tomatoes
.75-oz. pkg. garlic & herb salad
    dressing mix
2/3 to 1 c. water
cooked egg noodles

Heat oil in a skillet over medium heat. Add steak; brown on both
sides. Place steak, drippings and remaining ingredients in a slow
cooker. Add water to desired consistency. Cover and cook on low
setting for 8 to 10 hours. Serve over hot buttered noodles.
Serves 4 to 6.

Stir in a little quick-cooking tapioca with other ingredients
for a roast or stew...broth will thicken magically as it cooks!

Mom's Fall-Apart Sunday Roast
Karla Neese
Edmond, OK

My mom would always put this roast into the slow cooker early on Sunday mornings, before getting ready for church. When we came home from church around noon, the whole house smelled wonderful!

3-lb. boneless beef chuck roast
salt, pepper and garlic powder
   to taste
1 to 2 T. oil
4 to 6 potatoes, peeled and
   quartered

1 to 2 onions, quartered
3 to 4 carrots, peeled and cut
   into chunks
3 14-1/2 oz. cans green beans,
   drained and liquid reserved

Sprinkle roast generously with salt, pepper and garlic powder. Heat oil in a skillet; brown roast on all sides. Place potatoes in a slow cooker; place roast on top of potatoes. Add onions, carrots and green beans, sprinkling to taste with additional salt, pepper and garlic powder. Add enough of reserved liquid from beans to cover ingredients about halfway. Cover and cook on low setting for 6 to 8 hours. Serves 6.

All-day slow cooking works wonders on less-tender, inexpensive cuts of beef...arm and chuck roast, rump roast, short ribs, round steak and stew beef cook up juicy and delicious.

◆ Mouthwatering Roasts ◆
Like Mom used to make

Saucy Eye of Round

Sharon Demers
Dolores, CO

I combine any leftover beef and gravy with cooked vegetables to make a tasty beef pot pie.

1-1/2 lb. beef eye of round roast
10-1/2 oz. can beef broth
Optional: 1/4 c. white wine
1 T. soy sauce
1 T. catsup
1 T. mustard

1 T. dried, minced onion
1 clove garlic, minced
3 to 4 T. cornstarch
1/4 c. cold water
8-oz. pkg. sliced mushrooms

Place roast in a slow cooker; set aside. Mix broth, wine, if using, soy sauce, catsup, mustard, onion and garlic; pour over meat. Cover and cook on low setting for 6 to 8 hours. Thirty minutes before roast is done, dissolve cornstarch in water and stir into slow cooker. Stir in mushrooms; increase setting to high, cover and cook an additional 20 to 30 minutes. Makes 4 servings.

Slow-cook an extra-large roast for 2 tasty meals
in one...enjoy roast pork or beef the first night, then
serve shredded meat with barbecue sauce on buns
the next night!

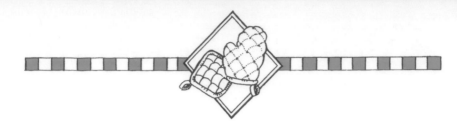

Apple Orchard Pork Roast

Marion Sundberg
Ramona, CA

A wonderful hearty meal.

2-lb. pork shoulder roast
1 T. oil
2 tart apples, cored, peeled
   and sliced
8 new redskin potatoes
1 onion, coarsely chopped

16-oz. pkg. baby carrots
10-3/4 oz. can cream of celery
   or mushroom soup
Worcestershire sauce to taste
salt and pepper to taste

Brown pork roast in oil on all sides; place in a slow cooker. Add apples and vegetables; top with remaining ingredients. Cover and cook on low setting for 7 to 8 hours, until meat is cooked through. Arrange meat and vegetables on a platter. Serve with cooking juices, thickened in a saucepan on the stove if needed. Makes 6 servings.

Slow-Cooked Pork Tenderloins

Connie Spangler
Palm Bay, FL

This couldn't be easier to fix!

2 1-lb. pork tenderloins
10-3/4 oz. can cream of
   mushroom soup
10-3/4 oz. can golden
   mushroom soup

10-3/4 oz. can French
   onion soup

Arrange tenderloins in a slow cooker. Whisk soups together in a bowl; pour over pork. Cover and cook on low setting for 4 to 5 hours, until meat is tender. Serves 4.

Teriyaki Pork Roast

Jane Gates
Saginaw, MI

My most-requested recipe!

3/4 c. apple juice
2 T. sugar
2 T. soy sauce
1 T. vinegar
1 t. ground ginger

1 t. garlic powder
1/4 t. pepper
2 to 3-lb. rolled pork loin roast
3 T. cold water
1-1/2 T. cornstarch

Combine apple juice, sugar, soy sauce, vinegar and seasonings in a slow cooker; mix well. Add roast and turn to coat; place fat-side up. Cover and cook on low setting for 7 to 8 hours, or on high setting for 3-1/2 to 4 hours. Shortly before serving, make gravy. Remove roast from slow cooker; place on a platter and keep warm. Strain cooking liquids from slow cooker into a small saucepan; skim fat if necessary. Bring to a boil. Combine water and cornstarch to make a paste; stir into boiling liquid. Cook and stir until thickened. Serve gravy with sliced roast. Makes 4 to 6 servings.

Cooking for a crowd? Roasting meats can easily be doubled in a large slow cooker. Add only half again as much seasoning, not twice as much...otherwise flavors may be too strong.

Jackie's Apple Corned Beef *Mary Lauff-Thompson*
Philadelphia, PA

*My friend gave me this recipe. I like to serve it with
Irish soda bread.*

8 new redskin potatoes
4 to 5 carrots, peeled and cut
    into chunks
1 onion, cut into 8 wedges
3-lb. corned beef brisket

4 c. apple juice
1 c. brown sugar, packed
1 T. Dijon or honey mustard

Arrange potatoes, carrots and onion wedges in a slow cooker; top
with corned beef. Stir together apple juice, brown sugar and mustard;
pour over top. Cover and cook on low setting for 8 to 10 hours. Slice
meat thinly across the grain. Serve with cooked vegetables, Sautéed
Cabbage and some of the cooking liquid. Makes 4 to 6 servings.

Sautéed Cabbage:

1/2 head cabbage, shredded
1/2 c. onion, chopped
1 to 2 cloves garlic, minced

1 to 2 T. butter
salt and pepper to taste

In a skillet over medium heat, sauté cabbage, onion and garlic in
butter until soft. Add salt and pepper to taste; serve warm.

Insert toothpicks into wedges of
cabbage or onion...they'll hold together during
slow cooking and can be served neatly.
Discard picks before serving.

Oktoberfest Pork Roast

Sherry Doherty
Medford, NJ

A real stick-to-your-ribs dinner that's perfect for a crisp autumn day.

3 to 4-lb. boneless pork roast
salt and pepper to taste
1 T. shortening
2 apples, cored, peeled and
    quartered

32-oz. pkg. sauerkraut
1 c. apple juice or water
Optional: 17-oz. pkg. fresh or
    frozen pierogies

Sprinkle roast with salt and pepper. Melt shortening in a skillet over high heat; brown roast on all sides. Place roast in slow cooker. Add apples, sauerkraut and juice or water; blend. Add pierogies, if using; push down gently to partially submerge them in the liquid. Cover and cook on low setting for 8 to 9 hours. Serves 4 to 6.

Trim off most of the fat from meat before slow cooking.
When meat is done, pour off juices into a bowl and let
stand for several minutes, then skim off fat as it rises to
the top. You'll get all of the flavor but less of the fat.

Orange-Glazed Cornish Hens

Jo Ann

A very special dinner for 2!

2 20-oz. Cornish game hens, thawed
salt and pepper to taste
8-oz. pkg. chicken-flavored stuffing mix, prepared
1 c. chicken broth

1 orange, sliced
1/4 c. orange juice
1/4 t. orange zest
2 T. honey
1 T. lemon juice
1-1/2 t. oil

Sprinkle hens inside and out with salt and pepper. Spoon prepared stuffing loosely into hens and truss closed. Place hens neck-end down in a large slow cooker. Stir together remaining ingredients; pour over hens. Cover and cook on low setting for 5 to 7 hours, basting once or twice with sauce in slow cooker, until juices run clear when pierced. Spoon sauce over hens to serve. Makes 2 servings.

Slow down and enjoy life.

-Eddie Cantor

Holiday Cranberry Pork Roast
Patricia Wissler
Harrisburg, PA

A delicious change from roast turkey.

2-1/2 to 3-lb. boneless
   pork roast
16-oz. can jellied cranberry
   sauce
1/2 c. cranberry juice cocktail
1/2 c. sugar

1 t. dry mustard
1/4 t. ground cloves
2 T. cornstarch
2 T. cold water
1 t. salt

Place pork roast in a slow cooker; set aside. Combine cranberry sauce, cranberry juice, sugar, mustard and cloves. Mix well and pour over roast. Cover and cook on low setting for 6 to 8 hours, or until tender. Remove roast from slow cooker; keep warm. To make gravy, skim fat from drippings in slow cooker. Measure 2 cups drippings, adding water if necessary. Pour into saucepan and bring to a boil over medium heat. Stir together cornstarch and cold water to make a paste; stir into drippings. Cook and stir until thickened; stir in salt. Serve gravy with sliced pork. Makes 4 to 6 servings.

Economical cuts of pork are perfect for slow cooking...
boneless shoulder roast, blade roast
and country-style ribs.

Rosemary & Thyme Chicken

Linda Sather
Corvallis, OR

My family loves this recipe...I use fresh herbs from my garden.

3-lb. roasting chicken
1 to 2 T. garlic, minced
kosher salt to taste
1/2 onion, sliced into wedges

4 sprigs fresh rosemary
3 sprigs fresh thyme
seasoning salt to taste

Rub inside of chicken with garlic and kosher salt. Stuff with onion wedges and herb sprigs. Sprinkle seasoning salt on the outside of chicken; place in slow cooker. Cover and cook on low setting for 8 to 10 hours. Serves 4.

Make gravy after a slow-cooked roast is done...it's easy. Set aside roast, leaving juices in the slow cooker. Stir up a smooth paste of 1/4 cup cold water and 1/4 cup cornstarch or all-purpose flour. Pour it into the slow cooker, stir well and set on high. In about 15 minutes, gravy will come to a boil...it's ready to serve!

◆ Mouthwatering Roasts ◆
Like Mom used to make

Bacon & Sage Roast Turkey
Jamie Johnson
Gooseberry Patch

The easiest-ever Thanksgiving dinner...all you need to add is cranberry sauce and dessert!

8 new redskin potatoes, halved
1-1/2 c. baby carrots
1/2 t. garlic-pepper seasoning
6-lb. turkey breast
12-oz. jar roast turkey gravy

2 T. all-purpose flour
4 to 6 slices bacon, crisply
  cooked and crumbled
1 T. Worcestershire sauce
3/4 t. dried sage

Arrange potatoes and carrots in a slow cooker; sprinkle with seasoning. Place turkey breast-side up on top of vegetables. In a small bowl, combine gravy, flour, bacon, Worcestershire sauce and sage. Mix well and pour over turkey and vegetables. Cover and cook on low setting for 7 to 9 hours, until juices run clear when pierced. Makes 8 servings.

When a slow-cooker roast recipe gives a range of cooking times like 8 to 10 hours, roasts will be tender after 8 hours and can be sliced neatly. After 10 hours, they will shred...perfect for sandwiches with sauce.

Party Cola Ham

Zoe Bennett
Columbia, SC

Delicious at gatherings any time of year! Serve either warm or cold.

3 to 4-lb. fully-cooked ham
1/2 c. brown sugar, packed

1 t. dry mustard
1/2 c. cola, divided

Cut a shallow diamond pattern in the surface of ham and set aside. Combine brown sugar and mustard; add enough cola to make a paste. Rub mixture over ham and place in slow cooker. Pour in remaining cola; cover and cook on high setting for one hour. Reduce to low setting and cook for 6 to 7 hours. Makes 8 to 12 servings.

Cider-Glazed Ham

Dana Cunningham
Lafayette, LA

We love this apple and spice-flavored ham!

3-lb. fully-cooked ham
4 c. apple cider or apple juice
1 c. brown sugar, packed
2 t. dry mustard

1/2 t. ground cloves
1/4 t. allspice
1/8 t. nutmeg

Place ham in a slow cooker; add enough cider or juice to cover. Top with remaining ingredients. Cover and cook on low setting for 10 to 12 hours. Makes 8 to 10 servings.

Tie rolled cloth napkins with ribbon and slip a fresh sprig
of sweet-scented thyme under the ribbon...charming!

7-Spice Sticky Chicken

Samantha Sparks
Madison, WI

This is so tender and good...pass the napkins, please!

3-lb. roasting chicken
4 t. salt
2 t. paprika
1 t. cayenne pepper
1 t. onion powder

1 t. dried thyme
1 t. white pepper
1/2 t. pepper
1/2 t. garlic powder
1 c. onion, chopped

Pat chicken dry inside and out with paper towels; set aside. Combine spices in a small bowl; mix well. Rub spice mixture well into chicken, inside and out. Place chicken in a large resealable zipping bag and refrigerate overnight. In the morning, place chicken in a slow cooker; top with chopped onion. Cover and cook on low setting for 8 to 10 hours. Serves 4 to 6.

Root vegetables like potatoes, carrots and onions grow tender and sweet with all-day slow cooking. Give sweet potatoes and parsnips a try too...delicious!

The Best Pot Roast Ever

*Joan Brochu
Hardwick, VT*

*This roast cooks up so tender in the slow cooker...
you'll love the gravy too.*

2 c. water
5 to 6-lb. beef pot roast
1-oz. pkg. ranch salad dressing
   mix
.7-oz. pkg. Italian salad dressing
   mix

.87-oz. pkg. brown gravy mix
6 to 8 potatoes, peeled and
   cubed
8 to 10 carrots, peeled and
   thickly sliced

Pour water into a large oval slow cooker; add roast. Combine mixes and sprinkle over roast. Cover and cook on low setting for 6 to 7 hours; add potatoes and carrots during the last 2 hours of cooking. Serves 6 to 8.

Turn leftover roast meat into a country-style pot pie. Cube meat and add a can or 2 of mixed veggies, a can of cream soup and seasonings to taste. Cover and cook on low for 4 to 6 hours. Top with refrigerated biscuits 30 minutes before serving time, cover and cook on low until biscuits are done. Mmm!

❖ Mouthwatering Roasts ❖
Like Mom used to make

Savory Merlot Pot Roast

Heather McClintock
Columbus, OH

This roast makes the house smell divine after a long day at work or a cold day of playing outside!

3 to 4-lb. beef chuck roast
1/2 t. meat tenderizer
pepper to taste
1 t. olive oil
10-3/4 oz. can cream of
    mushroom soup

1-1/2 oz. pkg. onion soup mix
1/2 c. merlot wine or beef broth
Optional: 1 T. cornstarch,
    2 T. cold water

Sprinkle roast on all sides with tenderizer and pepper. Heat oil over medium heat in a large non-stick skillet. Brown roast on all sides and transfer to a slow cooker. Combine soup, soup mix and wine or broth; pour over roast. Cover and cook on low setting for 6 to 8 hours. Remove roast to a serving platter; cover with aluminum foil to keep warm. If thicker gravy is desired, increase setting to high; mix cornstarch into water and stir into gravy in slow cooker. Cook, uncovered, for 10 to 20 minutes, until gravy reaches desired thickness. Serve gravy with roast. Serves 6 to 8.

Uh-oh...you forgot to thaw the roast overnight! Before placing the frozen roast in the crock, pour in a cup of warm water to cushion the crock. Add an extra 4 hours cooking time on low or 2 hours on high.

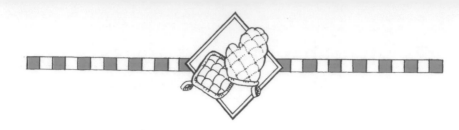

Sweet & Spicy Country Ham
Claire Bertram
Lexington, KY

This ham brings back memories of Christmas at Grandma's house.

6-lb. bone-in country ham
30 whole cloves
3 c. apple cider, divided
1 c. brown sugar, packed
1 c. maple syrup
2 T. cinnamon

2 T. ground cloves
1 T. nutmeg
2 t. ground ginger
zest of 1 orange
Optional: 1 T. vanilla extract

Score surface of ham with a knife and press whole cloves into ham; place in a slow cooker. Pour in cider to cover all except top 2 inches of ham. Pack brown sugar over top of ham, pressing firmly; drizzle with syrup. Sprinkle with spices, zest and vanilla, if using. Add remaining cider without going over fill line. Cover and cook on low setting for 8 to 10 hours. Makes 12 servings.

Table tents let everyone know what goodies are in potluck slow cookers! Fold a piece of paper in half and jot down or rubber stamp the recipe name on the front...be sure to add the cook's name.

❖ Mouthwatering Roasts ❖
Like Mom used to make

"Smoked" Beef Brisket

Joshua Logan
Corpus Christi, TX

So you've planned a cookout for tomorrow, but the weather forecast says rain? No problem...make this delicious smokey-tasting brisket in the slow cooker and have a picnic indoors!

2 to 4-lb. beef brisket or
   chuck roast
2 T. kosher salt
2 T. pepper, coarsely ground

2 cloves garlic, minced
2 T. smoke-flavored cooking
   sauce
Optional: barbecue sauce

Place meat in the center of a length of aluminum foil; rub all over with salt, pepper and garlic. Sprinkle cooking sauce over meat. Wrap aluminum foil around meat to cover completely; seal tightly. Place in a slow cooker; cover and cook on low setting for 8 to 10 hours. Unwrap meat; serve with juices from slow cooker or with barbecue sauce. Makes 4 to 6 servings.

Good to know. Set on low, a slow cooker uses
about as much energy as a 75-watt lightbulb...less than
an electric range uses!

Apple-Stuffed Turkey Breast

Dale Duncan
Waterloo, IA

*The combination of wild rice, apples and cranberries
really gives this turkey an amazing flavor.*

1-1/2 c. long grain & wild rice,
    uncooked
2 apples, peeled, cored and
    chopped
1 onion, finely chopped

1/2 c. sweetened dried
    cranberries
3 c. water
4 to 5-lb. boneless, skinless
    turkey breast

Combine rice, apples, onion and cranberries in a slow cooker; pour
water over top. Mix well. Place turkey on top of rice mixture. Cover
and cook on low setting for 8 to 9 hours. Serves 10.

All-day cooking on the low setting is preferred for
tougher cuts of meat...they'll turn out juicy
and fork-tender.

❖ Mouthwatering Roasts ❖
Like Mom used to make

Herb-Roasted Turkey

Tori Willis
Champaign, IL

A new way to prepare tender, delicious turkey...guests will love it!

5 to 6-lb. turkey breast
1/4 c. water
1/4 c. cream cheese, softened
2 T. butter, softened
1 T. soy sauce
1 green onion, finely chopped

1 clove garlic, finely chopped
1 T. fresh parsley, minced
1/2 t. dried basil
1/2 t. dried thyme
1/2 t. poultry seasoning
1/4 t. pepper

Place turkey breast-side up in a slow cooker; add water. Blend together remaining ingredients in a small bowl; spread over outside of turkey. Cover and cook on low setting for 8 to 10 hours, or on high setting for 4 to 6 hours. Makes 6 to 8 servings.

Not sure if the roast is done yet? Just check it with a meat thermometer. Recommended temperatures:

Chicken and turkey = 180 degrees,
Beef and pork = 160 degrees for medium,
170 degrees for well-done.

49

Lemony "Baked" Chicken

Sharon Lundberg
Longwood, FL

*Stir a little lemon zest and chopped parsley into steamed rice
for a perfect side dish.*

3 to 4-lb. roasting chicken	2 cloves garlic, minced
2 T. olive oil	1 t. dried parsley
1 lemon	salt and pepper to taste

Pat chicken dry with a paper towel; rub with oil. Put whole lemon
inside chicken; place in slow cooker. Sprinkle with garlic, parsley,
salt and pepper. Cover and cook on high setting for one hour. Turn to
low setting and cook an additional 6 to 7 hours. Makes 4 servings.

Tiny, tender new potatoes can simply be placed
on top of a roast...they'll steam to perfection while
the roast slow-cooks.

Italian Pot Roast

Kathy Dolge
Silver Spring, MD

*This is easy to toss together before I leave for work...my husband
likes it as much as I do!*

2 to 3-lb. beef chuck roast
1 T. oil
2 14-1/2 oz. cans Italian-style
   stewed tomatoes

4-oz. can sliced mushrooms,
   drained
Optional: cooked egg noodles
   or mashed potatoes

In a skillet over medium heat, brown roast in oil on both sides.
Place roast in a slow cooker; pour tomatoes over top. Cover and cook
on low setting for 10 to 11 hours. About 15 minutes before serving,
stir in mushrooms; cover and heat through. If desired, serve with
cooked egg noodles or potatoes. Makes 4 to 6 servings.

For perfect pasta, cook in boiling water just until tender,
then stir into the slow cooker during the last 30 minutes
of cooking time.

◈ Dinner in a Jiffy ◈
5 ingredients or less

Chicken Cordon Bleu

Debi Gilpin
Uniontown, PA

Prepare chicken rolls and refrigerate overnight...in the morning,
just pop 'em in the slow cooker and go!

4 to 6 boneless, skinless
   chicken breasts
4 to 6 thin slices cooked ham
4 to 6 slices Swiss cheese

10-3/4 oz. can cream of
   mushroom soup
1/4 c. milk

Place each chicken breast in a plastic zipping bag; pound to flatten.
Top each with a slice of ham and a slice of cheese; roll up and secure
with a toothpick. Arrange rolls in a slow cooker in layers. Mix soup
and milk; pour over chicken. Cover and cook on low setting for 4 to
6 hours, until chicken is no longer pink inside. To serve, remove
toothpicks and arrange chicken rolls on serving plate; spoon sauce
from slow cooker over rolls. Makes 4 to 6 servings.

A quick go-with for a slow-cooker meal...toss steamed
green beans, broccoli or zucchini with a little olive oil
and chopped fresh herbs.

St. Paddy's Corned Beef

*Connie West
Sonora, CA*

We enjoy this wonderful meal year 'round!

3 carrots, peeled and thickly
   sliced
3-lb. flat-cut corned beef brisket
   with seasoning packet

1 c. low-sodium beef broth
1/2 to 1 head cabbage, cut
   into wedges

Arrange carrots in the bottom of a slow cooker; place corned beef on top. Sprinkle with one-quarter of seasoning packet contents; discard rest of seasoning. Pour broth over all. Cover and cook on low setting for 8 to 10 hours, or on high setting for 5 to 6 hours. Add cabbage wedges, pushing down to moisten. Cover; cook on high setting for an additional 2 to 3 hours. Makes 8 to 10 servings.

Plug your slow cooker into an automatic timer if you need it to start cooking while you're away. Well-chilled foods can safely be held at room temperature for one to 2 hours.

◆ Dinner in a Jiffy ◆
5 ingredients or less

Easy Kielbasa Dinner

Denny Shaw
Drexel Hill, PA

There's nothing better than opening the door, smelling the delicious aroma and knowing my dinner is ready!

10 to 12 new redskin potatoes
16-oz. pkg. sauerkraut
1 t. caraway seed

1 T. light brown sugar, packed
1 lb. Kielbasa, cut into 2-inch
    pieces

Peel a strip around the middle of each potato; place potatoes in the bottom of a slow cooker. Place sauerkraut on top of potatoes; rinse sauerkraut bag with a little water and pour into slow cooker. Sprinkle caraway and brown sugar over sauerkraut; arrange Kielbasa pieces on top. Cover and cook on low setting for 8 to 10 hours. Serves 4.

Don't crack the crock! Sudden changes from cold to hot are a no-no. Don't set a hot crockery liner on a cold surface...run only warm, not cold, wash water into a hot crock.

Nacho Chicken & Rice

Candace Whitelock
Seaford, DE

Make wraps by spooning into flour tortillas, folding over and rolling up from the bottom.

1 lb. boneless, skinless
   chicken breasts, cubed
2 10-3/4 oz. cans Cheddar
   cheese soup

1-1/4 c. water
16-oz. jar chunky salsa
1-1/4 c. long-cooking rice,
   uncooked

Combine all ingredients in a slow cooker. Cover and cook on low setting for about 5 hours, or until chicken and rice are tender. Serves 6 to 8.

Prop a mini chalkboard next to the slow cooker...it's just right for announcing what's for dinner and what time it will be ready.

❖ Dinner in a Jiffy ❖
5 ingredients or less

4-Ingredient Chicken Chili
Stephanie Westfall
Dallas, GA

I like a lot of broth myself, but you may like a chunkier chili...just add broth to create the consistency you prefer.

4 boneless, skinless chicken
    breasts
8-oz. pkg. Monterey Jack cheese,
    cubed

16-oz. jar salsa
3 15-1/2 oz. cans Great
    Northern beans, drained
    and rinsed

Cover chicken breasts with water in a saucepan; simmer until cooked through, about 20 to 30 minutes. Reserve broth and shred chicken. Add reserved broth and chicken to a slow cooker; stir in cheese. Add salsa and beans to chicken mixture. Cover and cook on low setting for one to 2 hours, or until heated through and cheese is melted. Serves 4 to 6.

Fiesta Chicken Pronto
Kristi Duis
Maple Plain, MN

This is delicious served over rice! We like to shred the chicken and use it for tacos or burritos too.

8 boneless, skinless chicken
    breasts
16-oz. can black beans,
    drained and rinsed

10-3/4 oz. can cream of
    chicken soup
2 T. taco seasoning mix
1/4 c. salsa

Arrange chicken in a slow cooker. Combine remaining ingredients and pour over chicken. Cover and cook on high setting for 3 hours. Serves 8.

Keep a pair of long padded oven mitts nearby when slow cooking...they're perfect for lifting and carrying the hot crock safely.

Mom's Chicken Italiano

Ellen Lockhart
Roanoke, VA

My mother used this recipe often as I was growing up. Now I do too, thanks to a family recipe book that she and my mother-in-law put together. It's good over rice, sprinkled with grated Parmesan.

2 to 3 lbs. boneless, skinless
   chicken breasts
2 10-3/4 oz. cans golden
   mushroom soup

2 14-1/2 oz. cans diced
   tomatoes
1 c. onion, chopped
1 t. dried basil

Arrange chicken in a slow cooker. Mix together remaining ingredients and pour over chicken. Cover and cook on low setting for 8 hours. Cut or shred chicken into bite-size pieces before serving. Serves 4 to 6.

Cutting down on salt? Choose low-sodium canned soups, broth and veggies. You can also use garlic powder instead of garlic salt...just taste and adjust seasonings when food has finished cooking.

❖ Dinner in a Jiffy ❖
5 ingredients or less

Italian Sausage & Penne

Nancy Stizza-Ortega
Oklahoma City, OK

Pop some garlic bread in the oven...dinner is served!

3/4 lb. hot Italian sausage links,
   cut into bite-size pieces
1 red pepper, chopped

1/2 onion, chopped
26-oz. jar spaghetti sauce
6-oz. pkg. penne pasta, cooked

Stir together all ingredients except pasta in a slow cooker. Cover and cook on low setting for 7 to 8 hours. At serving time, stir in cooked pasta. Makes 4 servings.

A hearty dish like Italian Sausage & Penne
is perfect on a cool autumn night. Carry the crock right
out to your backyard picnic table and savor
the fall colors with your family!

Fix & Go Swiss Steak

Theresa Gilman
Kittery, ME

A scrumptious meal that couldn't be any easier!

1-1/2 lbs. boneless
    beef round steak, cut into
    serving-size pieces
1-1/2 oz. pkg. onion soup mix

2 14-1/2 oz. cans diced
    tomatoes
cooked rice

Arrange steak in a slow cooker; sprinkle with onion soup mix. Pour diced tomatoes over top. Cover and cook on high setting for 4 hours. Serve over rice. Makes 4 servings.

Joan's Chicken Stuffing Casserole

Joan Brochu
Hardwick, VT

Hearty and so filling, this chicken dish will be
the first to disappear at any potluck.

12-oz. pkg. chicken stuffing mix
3 10-3/4 oz. cans cream of
    chicken soup, divided
1/2 c. milk

3 to 4 c. cooked chicken, cubed
12-oz. pkg. shredded Cheddar
    cheese

Prepare stuffing mix according to package directions; place in a slow cooker. Stir in 2 cans soup. In a separate bowl, stir together remaining soup, milk and chicken. Add to slow cooker. Spread cheese over top. Cover and cook on low setting for 4 to 6 hours, or on high setting for 2 to 3 hours. Serves 6.

Be creative! Change flavors simply by substituting
a different cooking liquid. Try your favorite cream soup
or replace water with seasoned broth...just be sure
to add the same amount.

❖ Dinner in a Jiffy ❖
5 ingredients or less

Easy Special Pot Roast

Marge Dicton
Bartonsville, PA

This is one of my family's most-requested meals! It's so easy and makes a delicious gravy for egg noodles or potatoes. We like it anytime...it's especially great on cold, snowy winter days.

10-3/4 oz. can Cheddar
    cheese soup
10-3/4 oz. can golden
    mushroom soup

10-3/4 oz. can French
    onion soup
3-lb. beef chuck roast

Mix soups in a slow cooker; top with roast. Cover and cook on low setting for 8 to 9 hours, turning roast halfway through cooking time if possible. Makes 6 servings.

Place thick slices of onion under a beef roast for extra flavor...they'll also form a natural rack to keep the roast from cooking in its own fat.

Zesty Italian Chicken

Alice Ardaugh
Joliet, IL

Not your usual chicken dinner!

4 boneless, skinless chicken
   breasts
1/2 c. Italian salad dressing,
   divided

1/2 c. grated Parmesan cheese,
   divided
1 t. Italian seasoning, divided
4 potatoes, peeled and quartered

Arrange chicken in a slow cooker; sprinkle with half each of salad dressing, Parmesan and Italian seasoning. Add potatoes; top with remaining dressing, Parmesan and seasoning. Cover and cook on low setting for 8 hours, or on high setting for 4 hours. Serves 4.

Set up a mini salad bar at dinner! Fill the cups of a muffin tin with diced tomatoes, cucumbers and carrots plus a choice of dressings...family members can simply help themselves to toppings.

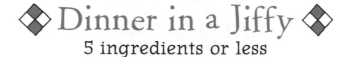

◆ Dinner in a Jiffy ◆
5 ingredients or less

Oh-So-Easy Lasagna

April Longmore
Preston, ID

Add a crisp tossed green salad...dinner is served!

1 to 2 lbs. ground beef,
   browned and drained
26-oz. jar Parmesan & Romano
   pasta sauce

8-oz. pkg. bowtie pasta, cooked
12-oz. container cottage cheese
16-oz. pkg. shredded mozzarella
   cheese

Mix together ground beef and pasta sauce. In a slow cooker, layer half each of ground beef mixture, pasta, cottage cheese and shredded cheese. Repeat with remaining ingredients. Cover and cook on low setting for 6 to 8 hours, or on high setting for 3 to 4 hours. Serves 8.

Take along the slow cooker on your next RV or camping trip! Put dinner on to cook in the morning, then sit down to a hearty home-cooked meal after a day of vacation fun.

Stuffed Game Hens

Lisa Bownas
Columbus, OH

If you like a crisper skin, just place roasted hens under the broiler for a few minutes.

2 20-oz. Cornish game hens, thawed
salt and pepper to taste

8-oz. pkg. chicken-flavored stuffing mix, prepared

Sprinkle hens all over with salt and pepper; stuff loosely with prepared stuffing. Wrap each hen tightly in a length of aluminum foil; arrange in slow cooker. Spoon any extra stuffing onto a length of foil and make a sealed packet; place on top of hens. Cover and cook on low setting for 12 hours, until juices run clear when pierced. Serves 2.

Not sure if your old slow cooker still heats properly?
It's simple to check. Fill it 2/3 full of water, cover
and cook on high setting for 4 hours. Check water
with an instant-read thermometer...if it reads
180 degrees, the slow cooker is working properly.

❖ Dinner in a Jiffy ❖
5 ingredients or less

Missy's Easy Pork Roast

Missy Frost
Xenia, OH

You won't believe how tender and delicious this roast is!
It's wonderful with mashed potatoes.

2 to 3-lb. pork roast
1-1/2 oz. pkg. onion soup mix

3/4 to 1 c. milk
2 slices bacon, halved

Place roast in a slow cooker; set aside. Mix together soup mix and milk and spread over roast. Lay bacon slices on top of roast. Cover and cook on low setting for 6 to 8 hours. Makes 4 to 6 servings.

Try a new side dish instead of rice or noodles...barley pilaf.
Simply prepare quick-cooking barley with chicken broth,
seasoned with a little chopped onion and dried parsley.
Filling, quick and tasty!

Creamy Chicken & Noodles

Melissa Dennis
Marysville, OH

We've shared this recipe with many other families...they love it too!

3 to 4 boneless, skinless
    chicken breasts
2 10-3/4 oz. cans cream of
    chicken soup

1/2 c. butter, sliced
4 10-1/2 oz. cans chicken broth
24-oz. pkg. frozen egg noodles

Combine first 4 ingredients in a slow cooker. Cover and cook on low setting for 8 hours. One hour before serving, remove chicken, shred and return to slow cooker. Stir in frozen noodles; cover and cook on low setting for one hour. Serve in soup bowls. Serves 4 to 6.

Fill a basket with the fixin's for a simple supper
like Creamy Chicken & Noodles and deliver to
new parents...how thoughtful!

Hearty Chick'n Dumplings

Jessica Ambrose
Oreland, PA

This is as good as Grandma used to make! Sometimes I'll add sliced celery or carrots too.

2 10-3/4 oz. cans cream of
     chicken soup
2 14-1/2 oz. cans chicken broth
1/2 onion, diced

1 lb. boneless, skinless
   chicken breasts
2 16.3-oz. tubes refrigerated
   biscuits, quartered

Combine first 3 ingredients in a slow cooker. Add chicken; cover and cook on high setting for 6 hours. During the last hour of cooking, remove chicken and shred with 2 forks; return to slow cooker. Add biscuit pieces to chicken mixture; stir to coat. Cover and cook on high setting for one hour. Serves 4.

We all have hometown appetites. Every other person is a bundle of longing for the simplicities of good taste once enjoyed on the farm or in the hometown he left behind.
-Clementine Paddleford

Spuds & Sausage Stew

Sue Gehr
Lititz, PA

This stew is a cinch to put together...the aroma while it's cooking instantly warms up the house on a cold day.

1 lb. smoked sausage, sliced
   3/4-inch thick
5 redskin potatoes, cut in
   1-inch cubes
4 carrots, peeled and cut in
   3/4-inch slices

10-3/4 oz. can cream of
   mushroom soup
Optional: 1 onion, sliced

Combine all ingredients in a slow cooker. Cover and cook on low setting for 6 to 8 hours. Makes 4 servings.

Get a head start by peeling and cutting up potatoes the night before. They won't turn dark if you cover them with water before refrigerating them.

Kielbasa & Red Beans

*Beth Schlieper
Lakewood, CO*

Serve over bowls of rice for traditional red beans & rice.

1 lb. Kielbasa, cut into
  bite-size pieces
4 to 5 15-1/2 oz. cans red beans
  or kidney beans, drained
  and rinsed

2 14-1/2 oz. cans diced
  tomatoes
1 onion, chopped
hot pepper sauce to taste

Combine all ingredients in a slow cooker. Cover and cook on low setting for 8 hours, or on high setting for 4 to 5 hours. Serves 6 to 8.

A wide roll of white freezer paper is oh-so-handy for covering party tables! Before dinner, kids can have fun drawing on it with crayons...after dinner, just toss the paper or display their masterpieces!

Roast Beef Hash

Carrie Bonikowske
Stevens Point, WI

Top each portion with a poached egg for an extra-hearty meal.

1-1/2 to 2 lbs. stew beef, cubed
20-oz. pkg. refrigerated
   shredded hashbrowns
1 onion, chopped

1/4 c. butter, melted
1 c. beef broth
salt and pepper to taste

Combine all ingredients in a slow cooker. Cover and cook on low setting for 6 to 8 hours. Serves 4 to 6.

Wake up to a hearty breakfast...simply fill up your
slow cooker with Roast Beef Hash before you
turn in for the night!

◈ Dinner in a Jiffy ◈
5 ingredients or less

Oniony Meatloaf

Billie Jo Behrendt
Stephenson, MI

No oats in the cupboard? Just substitute fine bread crumbs.

2 eggs
1/2 c. catsup
3/4 c. quick-cooking oats,
    uncooked

1-1/2 oz. pkg. onion soup mix
2 lbs. ground beef

Combine eggs, catsup, oats and soup mix in a large bowl. Add ground beef; mix well. Shape ground beef mixture into a round loaf. Cut three, 20"x3" strips of aluminum foil; crisscross strips to resemble spokes of a wheel. Place meatloaf in center of foil strips. Gently pull strips up and bend edges to form handles. Grasp foil handles and lift meatloaf into a slow cooker. Cover and cook on low setting for 5 hours, or until a meat thermometer reaches 160 degrees. Using foil strips as handles, remove meatloaf from slow cooker. Makes 8 servings.

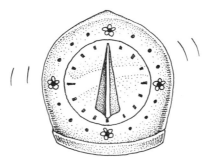

Speed up prep time on ground beef recipes! Brown several pounds of beef ahead of time, spoon into large plastic freezer bags and flatten to freeze. Thaw overnight in the fridge anytime it's needed.

Teriyaki Tri-Tip

Marion Sundberg
Ramona, CA

Tri-tip is a scrumptious California specialty...it's also known as triangle roast.

1-1/2 to 2-lb. beef tri-tip or
   rump roast, trimmed

15-oz. bottle teriyaki sauce
20-oz. can pineapple chunks

Place roast in a slow cooker. Pour teriyaki sauce over roast and top with pineapple. Cover and cook on low setting for 7 to 8 hours, or until meat shreds easily. Serves 4 to 6.

Pepper Steak

Ellen Sharp
Ashland, KY

Red pepper flakes and dried parsley are tasty additions.

1 lb. boneless beef round steak,
   cut into strips
2 green peppers, cut into strips
2 onions, sliced

2 14-1/2 oz. cans diced
   tomatoes
salt and pepper to taste

Combine all ingredients in a slow cooker. Cover and cook on low setting for 6-1/2 to 7 hours. Serves 4.

Garnishes make slow-cooked foods look extra delicious! Sprinkle on diced red peppers, minced chives or shredded cheese just before serving.

Pineapple Chicken

Tonya Lewis
Crothersville, IN

Very simple...very good!

6 boneless, skinless chicken breasts
salt, pepper and paprika to taste

20-oz. can pineapple tidbits, drained
2 T. Dijon mustard

Arrange chicken in a slow cooker; sprinkle with salt, pepper and paprika. Set aside. Mix together pineapple and mustard; spread over chicken. Cover and cook on high setting for 3 to 4 hours. Serves 6.

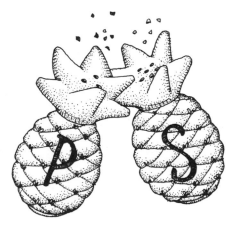

Simple slow-cooker recipes are ideal for older children just learning to cook. With supervision, they can learn to use paring knives, can openers and hot mitts...and they'll be oh-so-proud to serve the dinner they've prepared!

Country-Style Ribs & Redskins

Audrey Lett
Newark, DE

Try this recipe with thick pork chops too.

3 lbs. country-style pork ribs
1-1/2 lbs. new redskin potatoes

salt and pepper to taste
27-oz. can sauerkraut

Arrange ribs in a slow cooker; top with potatoes. Sprinkle with salt and pepper; spoon in sauerkraut. Cover and cook on low setting for 7 to 9 hours. Add salt and pepper to taste before serving, as needed. Serves 6.

Jump-start tomorrow's dinner! Chop and assemble ingredients tonight, refrigerating meat and veggies in separate containers. In the morning, toss everything in the slow cooker...you're set to go!

❖ Dinner in a Jiffy ❖
5 ingredients or less

One-Pot Ham Dinner

Michelle Rooney
Sunbury, OH

I like to keep a canned ham and canned veggies on hand...then this hearty meal can be tossed together in a pinch!

1-1/2 lbs. cooked ham, cubed
3 14-1/2 oz. cans green beans, drained and liquid reserved from one can

4 16-oz. cans whole new potatoes, drained and liquid reserved from one can
salt and pepper to taste

Combine ham, green beans, potatoes and reserved liquid in a slow cooker. Cover and cook on low setting for 6 to 7 hours. Add salt and pepper to taste. Serves 4 to 6.

If a dish that's nearly done seems too juicy, just take off the lid and turn the setting to high...excess liquid will evaporate quickly.

Lone Star BBQ Ribs

Gail Galipp
Mabank, TX

Use the barbecue sauce of your choice, like hickory or mesquite.

3 lbs. bone-in beef short ribs
1 c. water
1/2 c. barbecue sauce

1/2 c. dry red wine or beef broth
1 T. Worcestershire sauce

Arrange ribs in a slow cooker. Mix remaining ingredients together and pour over ribs. Cover and cook on low setting for 8 to 10 hours. Serves 4 to 6.

Cattle Drive Stew

Karen Pilcher
Burleson, TX

Yummy with cornbread!

1/2 lb. stew beef, cubed
16-oz. pkg. Kielbasa, sliced
1 onion, chopped

3 potatoes, peeled and chopped
28-oz. can baked beans

Arrange all ingredients in a slow cooker in the order shown. Cover and cook on high setting for 4 hours, or on low setting for 8 hours. Makes 6 to 8 servings.

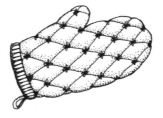

If you prefer grilled ribs, just place slow-cooked meat on a broiler pan...pop under the broiler for a few minutes, until they're slightly char-broiled and crisp.

Melting Pot

Flavorful meals from all over

Chicken Lasagna Florentine

Nicole Draves
Rockland, MA

This delicious recipe just looks complicated...it goes together really quickly, since you don't even need to boil the lasagna!

10-oz. pkg. frozen chopped spinach, thawed and drained
9-oz. pkg. frozen diced cooked chicken, thawed
2 10-3/4 oz. cans cream of chicken soup
8-oz. container sour cream
1 c. milk
1/2 c. grated Parmesan cheese
1/3 c. onion, chopped
1/2 t. salt
1/4 t. pepper
1/8 t. nutmeg
9 strips lasagna, uncooked and divided
1 c. shredded mozzarella cheese, divided

Combine all ingredients except lasagna and mozzarella in a large bowl; stir well and set aside. Arrange 3 uncooked lasagna strips in the bottom of a slow cooker sprayed with non-stick vegetable spray, breaking strips in half to fit. Spread 1/3 of spinach mixture over lasagna; sprinkle with 1/3 cup mozzarella. Layer with 3 more strips, half of remaining spinach mixture and 1/3 cup mozzarella. Top with remaining lasagna strips, spinach mixture and mozzarella. Cover and cook on high setting for one hour. Reduce to low setting and cook, covered, for 5 hours, or until lasagna is tender. Makes 8 servings.

Whether it's your grandmother's special recipe or one that's new to you, a slow cooker is the easy way to prepare savory long-simmering foods. Set aside one night a week to share new flavors with your family!

Easy Chicken Cacciatore

Sheryl Vinyard
Hillview, IL

Toss in a sliced green pepper, if you like.

4 boneless, skinless chicken
    breasts
4-oz. can sliced mushrooms,
    drained
1/2 c. water
26-oz. jar spaghetti sauce,
    divided

1 t. Italian seasoning
cooked spaghetti
Garnish: shredded mozzarella
    cheese

Arrange chicken in a slow cooker. Top with mushrooms, water and
half of sauce; sprinkle with seasoning. Cover and cook on low for
4 to 6 hours. At serving time, warm remaining sauce and toss with
cooked spaghetti. Top spaghetti with chicken; sprinkle with shredded
cheese. Serves 4.

Make whimsical placecards for a pasta dinner...write
guests' names on strips of uncooked lasagna,
broken to length.

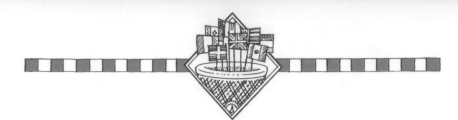

French Country Chicken

Teri Lindquist
Gurnee, IL

This recipe is completely my own and we really love it! It has a very fancy taste, yet takes only minutes to prepare. The white wine really makes this dish, but you can use chicken broth instead.

1 onion, chopped
6 carrots, peeled and sliced
   diagonally
6 stalks celery, sliced diagonally
6 boneless, skinless chicken
   breasts
1 t. dried tarragon
1 t. dried thyme

pepper to taste
10-3/4 oz. can cream of
   chicken soup
1-1/2 oz. pkg. onion soup mix
1/3 c. dry white wine or
   chicken broth
2 T. cornstarch
cooked rice or mashed potatoes

Combine onion, carrots and celery in the bottom of a slow cooker. Arrange chicken on top; sprinkle with seasonings. Mix together chicken soup and onion soup mix; spoon over chicken. Cover and cook on high setting for 4 hours, stirring after one hour. At serving time, stir together wine or broth and cornstarch; pour over chicken and mix well. Cook, uncovered, for an additional 10 minutes, until thickened. Stir again; serve over cooked rice or mashed potatoes. Makes 6 servings.

A single big blossom floating in a water-filled juice tumbler is a charming touch on the dinner table. Set one at each guest's place...sweet!

Company Beef Bourguignon

Melanie Lowe
Dover, DE

This dish is good enough to serve to guests! Sprinkle extra crumbled bacon over each portion, if you like.

3 lbs. boneless beef round
   steak, cubed
6 slices bacon, crisply cooked
   and crumbled, drippings
   reserved
1 onion, sliced
1 c. baby carrots
salt and pepper to taste
3 T. all-purpose flour
10-1/2 oz. can beef broth

1 T. tomato paste
2 cloves garlic, minced
1/2 t. dried thyme
1 bay leaf
16-oz. pkg. sliced mushrooms
1 T. oil
15-oz. jar pearl onions, drained
1/2 c. Burgundy wine or
   beef broth

Brown beef cubes in reserved bacon drippings; place in a slow cooker. Add onion, carrots, salt and pepper to skillet; stir in flour. Add broth and tomato paste; mix well and pour over beef. Sprinkle bacon, garlic and herbs over beef. Cover and cook on low setting for 8 to 10 hours. One hour before serving, sauté mushrooms in oil; add to slow cooker along with pearl onions and wine or broth. Discard bay leaf. Makes 4 to 6 servings.

Add tender fresh veggies like tomatoes and zucchini
near the end of cooking time...they'll stay firm
and brightly colored.

Polish Pepper Pot

Karen Pilcher
Burleson, TX

So hearty...really sticks to your ribs!

5 to 6 slices bacon, diced
5 to 6 slices bologna, chopped
5 to 6 slices salami, chopped
5 hot dogs, sliced
4 redskin potatoes, peeled
   and cubed
1 yellow onion, chopped

1 clove garlic, pressed
1 green pepper, chopped
28-oz. can stewed tomatoes
1 T. hot pepper sauce
1/2 t. seasoned salt
1/4 t. pepper

Combine all ingredients together in a large skillet over medium heat. Sauté until bacon is cooked through. Drain; spoon into a slow cooker. Cover and cook on low setting for 3 hours. Makes 4 to 5 servings.

Invite friends right into the kitchen and serve up
hot food directly from a slow cooker on the countertop.
For extra serving space, simply place a large cutting
board over the sink.

Lithuanian Chicken

Ginger Wunderlich
Demorest, GA

This recipe was given to me years ago by an old friend. It's even better the second day...if there is any left!

2 14-1/2 oz. cans sauerkraut,
    drained and rinsed
1/4 c. tomato paste
1/2 onion, sliced
4 stalks celery, diced
1 clove garlic, minced

4 to 5 lbs. boneless, skinless
    chicken breasts
3 c. water
1 t. salt
1/4 c. pine nuts or slivered
    almonds

Combine sauerkraut, tomato paste, onion, celery and garlic in a slow cooker. Cover and cook for one hour on high setting. Reduce to low setting; cover and cook for an additional one to 2 hours. Meanwhile, simmer chicken in water and salt until tender, about 20 to 30 minutes. Drain chicken and cut into bite-size pieces. Add chicken to slow cooker; cover and cook on low setting for an additional 30 minutes. Sprinkle with nuts at serving time. Makes 6 servings.

Slow cooking at high altitude takes a little longer. Be sure to allow an extra 30 minutes for each hour of cooking time specified in the recipe.

Swedish Cabbage Rolls

Linda Sinclair
Valencia, CA

Comfort food...just like Mom used to make.

12 large leaves cabbage
1 egg, beaten
1/4 c. milk
1/4 c. onion, finely chopped
1 t. salt
1/4 t. pepper
1/2 lb. ground beef

1/2 lb. ground pork
1 c. cooked rice
8-oz. can tomato sauce
1 T. brown sugar, packed
1 T. lemon juice
1 t. Worcestershire sauce
Garnish: sour cream

Immerse cabbage leaves in a large kettle of boiling water for about 3 minutes, or until limp; drain well and set aside. Combine egg, milk, onion, salt, pepper, beef, pork and cooked rice; mix well. Place about 1/4 cup meat mixture in the center of each leaf; fold in sides and roll ends over meat. Arrange cabbage rolls in a slow cooker. Combine remaining ingredients and pour over rolls. Cover and cook on low setting for 7 to 9 hours. Spoon sauce over rolls and garnish with sour cream. Makes 6 servings.

New luggage tags make fun placecards...they'll put guests right in the mood to try new foods from faraway places!

German Sauerbraten

Lenore Mincher
Patchogue, NY

Serve with spaetzle noodles tossed with butter.

4 to 5-lb. beef rump roast
2 t. salt
1 t. ground ginger
2-1/2 c. water
2 c. cider vinegar
2 onions, sliced
1/3 c. sugar

2 T. pickling spice
1 t. whole peppercorns
8 whole cloves
2 bay leaves
2 T. oil
16 to 20 gingersnaps, crushed

Rub roast all over with salt and ginger; place in a deep glass bowl and set aside. Combine water, vinegar, onions, sugar and spices in a saucepan; bring to a boil. Pour over roast; turn to coat. Cover roast and refrigerate for 3 days, turning twice each day. Remove roast, reserving marinade; pat dry. Heat oil in a Dutch oven; brown roast on all sides. Place roast in a slow cooker. Strain marinade, reserving half of onions and spices. Pour 1-1/2 cups marinade, onions and spices over roast; refrigerate remaining marinade. Cover and cook on low setting for 6 to 7 hours, until roast is tender. Remove roast to platter; keep warm. Discard onions and spices; add enough of refrigerated marinade to slow cooker to equal 3-1/2 cups. Pour into a saucepan; bring to a boil. Add crushed gingersnaps; simmer until gravy thickens. Slice roast; serve with gravy. Makes 12 to 14 servings.

Garden-fresh herbs are delicious...if you have them on hand, just use double the amount of dried herbs called for in a recipe.

Southwestern Pork Chalupas   *Vickie*

For a speedier start, simply use 2 to 3, 15-ounce cans of pinto beans.

16-oz. pkg. dried pinto beans
4 c. water
4-oz. can chopped green chiles
2 T. chili powder
2 t. ground cumin
1 t. dried oregano
salt and pepper to taste
4-lb. pork shoulder roast
16-oz. pkg. corn chips
Garnish: shredded Mexican-
    blend cheese, sour cream,
    salsa

Cover beans with water in a large soup pot; soak overnight. Drain.
Combine beans, water, chiles and spices in a slow cooker; mix well.
Add roast; cover and cook on low setting for 4 hours. Remove roast
and shred, discarding any bones; return pork to slow cooker. Cover
and cook on low setting for an additional 2 to 4 hours, adding more
water if necessary. At serving time, arrange corn chips on serving
plates. Spoon pork mixture over chips; garnish as desired. Serves 8.

Fiesta Beef Enchiladas   *Jane Terrill*
Cookson, OK

Garnish with sliced avocado.

1 to 2 lbs. ground beef,
    browned and drained
1 onion, chopped
10-oz. can mild enchilada sauce
4-oz. can diced green chiles
2 10-3/4 oz. cans Cheddar
    cheese soup
10-3/4 oz. can cream of
    chicken soup
10-3/4 oz. can cream of
    mushroom soup
12 6-inch corn tortillas, torn
    into bite-size pieces

Combine all ingredients except tortillas in a slow cooker; mix well.
Cover and cook on low setting for 8 to 10 hours, or on high setting for
4 hours. Stir in tortillas one hour before serving time. Serves 6.

Melting Pot
Flavorful meals from all over

Mexican Albondigas Soup

Sherry Sheehan
Phoenix, AZ

My Hispanic pastor tells me this tasty slow-cooker soup tastes just like the soup his mother used to make.

2 lbs. lean ground beef
1 c. Italian-seasoned dry
    bread crumbs
1 egg, beaten
Optional: 1/4 c. olive oil
3 stalks celery, sliced
1 green pepper, diced
1 c. carrots, peeled and diced
15-1/4 oz. can corn, drained
2 14-oz. cans beef broth
10-oz. can diced tomatoes
    with chiles

4-oz. can diced green chiles
3 c. cooked rice
2 T. fresh cilantro, finely
    chopped
2 T. onion, minced
1 t. garlic powder
1 t. ground cumin
1 t. chili powder
1 t. salt
1/2 t. pepper
4 to 5 c. water

Combine ground beef, bread crumbs and egg; form into one-inch balls. Brown in a skillet over medium heat, adding oil if desired; drain. Place meatballs in a slow cooker and set aside. In a small saucepan, cover celery, green pepper and carrots with a little water. Cook until tender; add to slow cooker with remaining ingredients. Cover and cook on low setting for 3 to 4 hours. Serves 8.

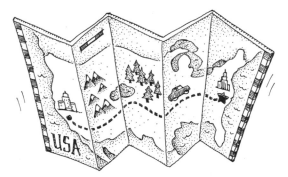

Paper fold-out maps make fun table coverings! Pick them up for a song at a thrift store or used book store...cover with a clear plastic tablecloth if you like.

Jammin' Jambalaya

Valarie Dennard
Palatka, FL

Yum! This feeds a crowd...and everybody loves it!

1 lb. boneless, skinless chicken
    breasts, cubed
1 lb. andouille sausage, sliced
28-oz. can diced tomatoes
1 onion, chopped
1 green pepper, chopped
1 c. celery, chopped
1 c. chicken broth

2 t. Cajun seasoning
2 t. dried oregano
2 t. dried parsley
1 t. cayenne pepper
1/2 t. dried thyme
1 lb. frozen cooked shrimp,
    thawed and tails removed
cooked rice

Place chicken, sausage, tomatoes, onion, pepper, celery and broth
in a slow cooker. Stir in seasonings; mix well. Cover and cook for 7 to
8 hours on low setting, or 3 to 4 hours on high setting. Add shrimp
during final 30 minutes of cooking time. Serve over cooked rice.
Makes 10 to 12 servings.

Maple Praline Chicken

Jill Valentine
Jackson, TN

Any day is Mardi Gras when you serve this delicious chicken!

6 boneless, skinless
    chicken breasts
2 T. Cajun seasoning
1/4 c. butter, melted
1/2 c. maple syrup

2 T. brown sugar, packed
1 c. chopped pecans
6-oz. pkg. long-grain and wild
    rice, cooked

Sprinkle chicken with Cajun seasoning. In a skillet over medium-high
heat, cook chicken in butter until golden. Arrange chicken in a slow
cooker. Mix together syrup, brown sugar and pecans; pour over
chicken. Cover and cook on low setting for 6 to 8 hours. Serve with
cooked rice. Makes 6 servings.

Country Captain

Marlene Darnell
Newport Beach, CA

*We discovered this curry-flavored dish with the unusual name
on a trip to southern Georgia.*

2 T. olive oil
3-lb. chicken, quartered and
   skin removed
2 cloves garlic, minced
1 onion, chopped
1 green pepper, chopped
1/2 c. celery, chopped
2 t. curry powder

1/3 c. currants or raisins
14-1/2 oz. can whole tomatoes,
   chopped
1 t. sugar
salt and pepper to taste
cooked rice
Garnish: 1/4 c. slivered almonds

Heat oil in a skillet over medium heat. Sauté chicken just until golden;
place in slow cooker and set aside. Add garlic, onion, green pepper,
celery and curry powder to skillet; sauté briefly. Remove from heat;
stir in remaining ingredients except rice and almonds. Pour over
chicken. Cover and cook on low setting for 6 hours, until chicken is
no longer pink. Serve over cooked rice; sprinkle with almonds.
Makes 4 servings.

Host an adventure potluck! Ask each guest to bring
a favorite dish from "back home"...whether that's
somewhere across the USA or even around the world.

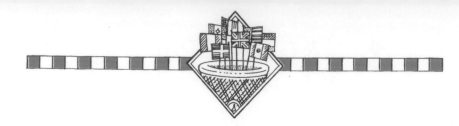

My Brother's Seafood Paella

Pamela Berry
Huntington, IN

*My brother, who does all the cooking for his family, shared
this delicious recipe with me.*

1 c. long-cooking rice, uncooked
2 c. water
1 onion, diced
14-1/2 oz. can diced tomatoes
3 cloves garlic, minced
1 t. salt
1 t. pepper
1/8 t. saffron

Optional: 1/4 t. cayenne pepper
1/2 lb. mild fish fillets, cut into
    1-inch cubes
1/2 lb. scallops
1/2 lb. medium shrimp, peeled
    and cleaned
8-oz. pkg. frozen peas, thawed
Garnish: 1 lemon, quartered

Combine rice, water, onion, tomatoes, garlic and seasonings in a
slow cooker; mix thoroughly. Cover and cook on high setting for 2 to
3 hours. Add fish, scallops, shrimp and peas; cover and cook on high
for an additional hour. Serve with lemon wedges. Makes 4 servings.

A slow cooker is oh-so handy, but don't use it
to reheat cooked foods...it just doesn't warm up
quickly enough. Instead, simmer on the stovetop or
place in the microwave for a few minutes, until bubbly.

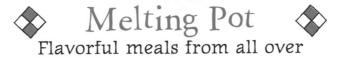

Melting Pot
Flavorful meals from all over

Arroz con Pollo

Michelle Sheridan
Huntsville, AL

Chicken and rice with a Spanish accent!

1/4 t. saffron
2 T. boiling water
3 lbs. boneless, skinless chicken
    breasts
1 T. oil
2 onions, finely chopped
4 cloves garlic, minced
1 t. salt
1/4 t. pepper
1-1/2 c. long-cooking rice,
    uncooked

28-oz. can whole tomatoes,
    chopped
1 c. chicken broth
1/2 c. dry white wine or
    chicken broth
1 green pepper, finely chopped
1 c. frozen green peas, thawed
Garnish: sliced green olives
    with pimentos
Optional: hot pepper sauce

Combine saffron and boiling water in a cup; set aside. In a skillet over medium-high heat, cook chicken in oil just until golden. Place chicken in a slow cooker and set aside. Add onions to skillet. Reduce heat to medium; cook and stir until softened. Add garlic, salt and pepper; cook and stir for one minute. Add rice; cook and stir until coated. Add saffron mixture, tomatoes, broth and wine or broth; pour over chicken. Cover and cook on low setting for 6 to 8 hours, until chicken juices run clear and rice is tender. Increase heat to high; add green pepper and peas. Cover and cook an additional 20 minutes. Garnish with olives; serve with hot sauce, if desired. Makes 6 servings.

Keep frozen chopped onions, peppers and veggie blends on hand for quick slow-cooker meal prep. They'll thaw quickly so you can assemble a recipe in a snap...no peeling, chopping or dicing!

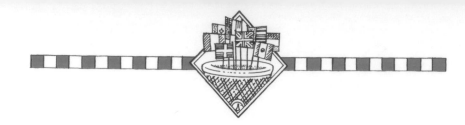

Slow-Cooker Cassoulet

Jennifer Denny
Delaware, OH

Use Kielbasa instead of Italian sausage, if you like.

1/2 lb. cooked ham, cubed
1/2 lb. Italian sausage, cooked
   and diced
1 onion, diced
3 16-oz. cans navy beans,
   drained and rinsed
8-oz. can tomato sauce

1/4 c. water
1/4 c. catsup
2 T. brown sugar, packed
1/2 t. salt
1/2 t. dry mustard
1/4 t. pepper

Combine all ingredients in a slow cooker; mix well. Cover and cook on low setting for 2 to 3 hours, until hot and bubbly. Serves 4 to 6.

Coq Au Vin

Kendall Hale
Lynn, MA

Elegant enough for guests.

4 boneless, skinless chicken
   breasts
16-oz. pkg. sliced mushrooms
15-oz. jar pearl onions, drained
1/2 c. dry white wine or
   chicken broth

1 t. dried thyme
1 bay leaf
1 c. chicken broth
1/3 c. all-purpose flour
cooked rice
Garnish: fresh parsley, chopped

Place chicken in a slow cooker; top with mushrooms and onions. Drizzle with wine and sprinkle thyme over top; add bay leaf. Stir together broth and flour; pour into slow cooker. Cover and cook on low setting for 5 hours, until chicken juices run clear. Discard bay leaf. Serve over rice; sprinkle with parsley. Makes 4 servings.

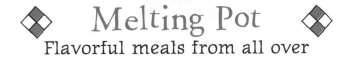

Pork Marengo

Penny Sherman
Cumming, GA

In a hurry? Don't brown the meat and onions...it will still be tasty!

2 lbs. boneless pork shoulder,
    cubed
1 yellow onion, chopped
2 T. oil
14-1/2 oz. can diced tomatoes
1 c. sliced mushrooms
1 t. chicken bouillon granules

1 t. dried marjoram
1/2 t. dried thyme
1/8 t. pepper
1/3 c. cold water
3 T. all-purpose flour
salt and pepper to taste
cooked rice or pasta

In a skillet over medium heat, cook pork cubes and onion in oil until browned. Drain and place in slow cooker; set aside. Place tomatoes, mushrooms, bouillon and seasonings in skillet; cook and stir briefly, scraping up bits from bottom of skillet. Pour over pork. Cover and cook on low setting for 8 hours. Blend water into flour; stir into pork. Add salt and pepper to taste. Increase heat to high setting and cook, uncovered, for 15 to 20 minutes, until thickened, stirring occasionally. Serve over cooked rice or pasta. Makes 4 servings.

When the kids study another country in school, why not try out a food from that country? Let them help choose a recipe and shop for the ingredients...they'll learn so much and have fun doing it!

Irish Beef Stew

Stacie Avner
Delaware, OH

So easy!

2 lbs. stew beef, cubed
1-1/2 oz. pkg. onion soup mix
2 c. carrots, peeled and cubed
2 c. potatoes, peeled and cubed

2 10-3/4 cans tomato soup
1-1/3 c. water
1 t. salt
1/2 t. pepper

Combine all ingredients in a slow cooker; mix well. Cover and cook on low setting for 8 to 10 hours. Serves 8.

Flemish Beef Stew

Geneva Rogers
Gillette, WY

Makes lots of yummy gravy…good spooned over barley pilaf.

2 lbs. boneless beef round
    steak, cubed
1 T. oil
3/4 lb. sliced mushrooms
3 T. all-purpose flour
2 c. dark beer or beef broth
4 carrots, peeled and cut into
    1-inch pieces

1 onion, chopped
1 clove garlic, chopped
1-1/2 T. Dijon mustard
1 t. caraway seed
3/4 t. salt
1/2 t. pepper
1 bay leaf

In a skillet over medium heat, brown beef cubes in oil. Drain beef; place in a slow cooker and set aside. Add mushrooms to skillet; cook and stir for 5 to 7 minutes. Sprinkle flour over mushrooms. Cook without stirring for 10 seconds; cook and stir for another 30 seconds. Add beer or broth to skillet; cook and whisk for about 3 minutes, until bubbly and thickened. Spoon mushroom mixture over beef; add remaining ingredients. Cover and cook on low setting for 8 hours, until beef is very tender. Discard bay leaf. Serves 8.

Brachiola Stuffed Beef

Joan Brochu
Hardwick, VT

If you've never tried this, you don't know what you're missing!

2 lbs. boneless beef round steak
1/2 c. seasoned bread crumbs
1/2 c. grated Parmesan cheese
1 T. garlic, minced
1 egg, beaten
1/4 t. pepper

2 eggs, hard-boiled, peeled
  and sieved
32-oz. jar meatless spaghetti
  sauce, divided
cooked linguine pasta

Place steak between 2 lengths of wax paper; pound until thin and set aside. Mix together bread crumbs, cheese, garlic, egg, pepper and sieved eggs; spread over steak. Roll up steak and tie at one-inch intervals with kitchen string. Spread one cup spaghetti sauce in the bottom of a slow cooker; set a rack on top. Place rolled-up steak on rack; cover with remaining sauce. Cover and cook on low setting for 6 to 8 hours, until steak is very tender. Slice between strings and serve on hot linguine. Makes 6 servings.

Good company in a journey
makes the way seem shorter.
-Izaak Walton

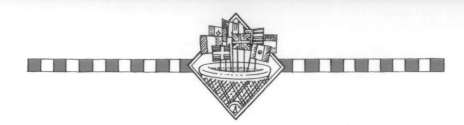

Russian Beef Borscht

Rita Morgan
Pueblo, CO

Serve in big soup bowls, dolloped with sour cream...there's nothing better on a cold day!

4 c. cabbage, thinly sliced
1-1/2 lbs. beets, peeled
    and grated
5 carrots, peeled and sliced
1 parsnip, peeled and sliced
1 c. onion, chopped
1 lb. stew beef, cubed

4 cloves garlic, minced
14-1/2 oz. can diced tomatoes
3 14-1/2 oz. cans beef broth
1/4 c. lemon juice
1 T. sugar
1 t. pepper

In a slow cooker, layer ingredients in order given. Cover and cook on low setting for 7 to 9 hours, just until vegetables are tender. Makes 8 to 10 servings.

Easy does it! Scrub the crockery liner gently...a nylon scrubbie is just right for removing cooked-on food particles.

Chinese-Style BBQ Pork

Ruth Leonard
Columbus, OH

We ate this roast pork when we lived in China. Serve it with steamed rice and stir-fried veggies like broccoli, carrots and peppers.

2-lb. boneless pork roast
1/4 c. soy sauce
1/4 c. hoisin sauce
3 T. catsup
3 T. honey
2 t. garlic, minced

2 t. fresh ginger, peeled
  and grated
1 t. dark sesame oil
1/2 t. Chinese 5-spice powder
1/2 c. chicken broth

Place roast in a large plastic zipping bag and set aside. In a small bowl, whisk together remaining ingredients except broth; pour over roast. Seal bag; refrigerate at least 2 hours, turning occasionally. Place roast in a slow cooker; pour marinade from bag over roast. Cover and cook on low setting for 8 hours. Remove pork from slow cooker; keep warm. Add broth to liquid in slow cooker; cover and cook on low setting for 30 minutes, or until thickened. Shred pork with 2 forks and stir into sauce in slow cooker. Serves 6.

Create a fresh-tasting, crunchy salad your family will love! Simply toss together packaged coleslaw mix with add-ins like raisins, dried cranberries or cheese crumbles and bottled salad dressing.

Cantonese Dinner

Lisa Ludwig
Fort Wayne, IN

*This recipe is a family favorite. Whether served over rice or
chow mein noodles, it's full of flavor!*

1-1/2 to 2 lbs. boneless beef
   round steak, cut into strips
1 T. oil
1 onion, chopped
1 green pepper, chopped
3/4 lb. sliced mushrooms

8-oz. can tomato sauce
3 T. brown sugar, packed
1-1/2 T. vinegar
1-1/2 t. salt
2 t. Worcestershire sauce

In a skillet over medium heat, brown beef strips in oil; drain. Place
beef, onion, green pepper and mushrooms in a slow cooker. Combine
remaining ingredients and mix well; pour over meat and vegetables.
Cover and cook on low setting for 6 to 8 hours, or on high setting for
3 hours. Serves 4.

Orange Teriyaki Chicken

Tina Goodpasture
Meadowview, VA

Who would guess that the secret ingredient is orange marmalade?

1-1/2 c. chicken broth
1/2 c. teriyaki sauce
1/2 c. green onion, sliced
   and divided
3 cloves garlic, minced
3/4 c. orange marmalade

2 T. cornstarch
8 boneless, skinless
   chicken thighs
cooked rice
1/2 c. walnuts, coarsely chopped

Mix broth, sauce, 1/4 cup onion, garlic, marmalade and cornstarch
in a slow cooker. Add chicken; turn to coat. Cover and cook on low
setting for 8 to 9 hours. Serve over rice, garnished with walnuts and
remaining onion. Makes 4 to 6 servings.

Chilis, Chowders, Soups & Stews

Supper in a soup bowl

White Bean Chicken Chili

Lori Crawford
Sebring, FL

Pick up a roast chicken from the deli to get a head start on this delicious chili.

2 T. oil
1 onion, chopped
2 cloves garlic, minced
1 lb. cooked chicken, diced
2 14-1/2 oz. cans diced
    tomatoes
16-oz. can Great Northern
    beans, drained and rinsed
10-oz. can tomatoes with chiles
1-1/2 c. water

2 cubes chicken bouillon
1/2 t. dried oregano
1/2 t. coriander
1/4 t. ground cumin
salt and pepper to taste
Garnish: sour cream, shredded
    Cheddar cheese, sliced black
    olives, diced avocado,
    tortilla chips

Heat oil in a skillet over medium heat; cook onion and garlic until soft. Place in a slow cooker with remaining ingredients except garnish. Cover and cook on low setting for about 4 hours. Garnish portions as desired. Makes 8 to 10 servings.

Host a neighborhood chili cook-off. Invite everyone to bring slow cookers filled with their own special chili...you provide yummy toppings and cornbread on the side. Have a prize for the winner!

Chilis, Chowders, Soups & Stews
◆◆ Supper in a soup bowl ◆◆

Vegetarian Cincinnati Chili

Leath Sarvo
Cincinnati, OH

A meatless version of a local tradition! Serve over cooked spaghetti for 2-way chili or topped with shredded cheese for 3-way chili.

46-oz. can tomato juice
16-oz. can kidney beans,
   drained and rinsed
1 onion, chopped
2 T. chili powder
1-1/2 t. white vinegar
1 t. allspice

1 t. cinnamon
1 t. pepper
1 t. ground cumin
1/8 t. garlic powder
1/4 t. Worcestershire sauce
5 bay leaves

Combine all ingredients in a slow cooker. Cover and cook on low setting for 5 hours. Discard bay leaves before serving. Serves 6.

Joan's Chili

Joan Shearman
Toledo, OH

I like to make this a day in advance so the spicy flavors can mingle, then reheat it on the stovetop the next day to serve with crackers.

2 lbs. ground beef
1 onion, chopped
1 t. garlic, minced
1 green pepper, chopped
2 stalks celery, chopped
2 to 3 15-1/2 oz. cans kidney
   beans, drained and rinsed
28-oz. can diced tomatoes

15-oz. can tomato sauce
1-1/2 T. sugar
1-1/4 T. chili powder
2 t. salt
1/4 t. cayenne pepper
1/4 t. paprika
1 t. dried basil
1 bay leaf

Brown ground beef, onion and garlic in a skillet; drain. Combine with remaining ingredients in a slow cooker. Cover and cook on low setting for 8 hours. Discard bay leaf before serving. Serves 8 to 10.

Creamy Broccoli Soup

Angela Britton
Moss Point, MS

A favorite, made zippier with Mexican cheese!

1 c. onion, chopped
1/2 c. butter
3 12-oz. cans evaporated milk
2 10-oz. pkgs. frozen broccoli, cooked

3 10-3/4 oz. cans cream of mushroom soup
16-oz. jar Mexican pasteurized process cheese sauce

Sauté onion in butter until tender; spoon into a slow cooker. Stir in remaining ingredients. Cover and cook on low setting for 2 to 3 hours, until heated through. Serves 4 to 6.

Carol's Cheesy Potato Soup

Carol McCullough
Waterloo, IA

This is a variation on my scalloped potato recipe...I love it!

2-1/2 lbs. russet potatoes, peeled and cubed
1 c. cooked ham, cubed
3 to 4 green onions, sliced
2 10-3/4 oz. cans cream of chicken soup
10-3/4 oz. can cream of mushroom soup

8-oz. container sour cream with chives
8-oz. container sour cream
2 to 3 c. finely shredded mild Cheddar cheese
salt and pepper to taste

Cover potatoes with water in a saucepan. Bring to a boil; reduce heat and simmer until tender. Place potatoes and cooking water in a slow cooker; add remaining ingredients except salt and pepper. Stir well; cover and cook on high setting for 2 to 3 hours, or on low setting for 4 to 6 hours. Add salt and pepper to taste. Makes 6 to 8 servings.

Chilis, Chowders, Soups & Stews
◆ Supper in a soup bowl ◆

Creamy Tomato Soup

Flo Burtnett
Gage, OK

The perfect partner for a grilled cheese sandwich!

1 onion, chopped
2 T. margarine
2 14-1/2 oz. cans diced
   tomatoes
2 10-3/4 oz. cans tomato soup
1-1/2 c. milk
1 t. sugar

1/2 t. dried basil
1/2 t. paprika
1/8 t. garlic powder
8-oz. pkg. cream cheese,
   cubed and softened
Optional: croutons

In a large saucepan over medium heat, sauté onion in margarine
until tender. Stir in remaining ingredients except cream cheese
and croutons; bring to a boil. Reduce heat; cover and simmer for
10 minutes. Stir in cream cheese and heat until melted. Serve
immediately, garnished with croutons if desired. Makes 8 servings.

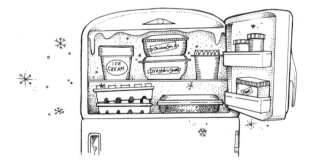

How comforting to have a freezer full of delicious soup!
Whenever you make a favorite slow-cooker soup recipe,
simply double it and freeze half in a freezer-safe
container. Thaw overnight in the fridge and
heat 'til bubbly on the stove.

Turkey & Wild Rice Soup

Judith Jennings
Ironwood, MI

This hearty soup is chock-full of veggies! Make it even healthier by using fat-free broth and evaporated milk, if you wish.

2 t. oil
1/2 c. onion, chopped
1 c. deli smoked turkey, diced
1 c. celery, diced
1 c. carrots, peeled and diced
1/2 c. long-cooking wild rice,
    uncooked

1 t. dried tarragon
1/4 t. pepper
2 14-oz. cans chicken broth
12-oz. can evaporated milk
1/3 c. all-purpose flour
1 c. frozen peas, thawed
Optional: 2 T. dry sherry

Heat oil in a skillet over medium heat. Cook onion for about 4 minutes until tender, stirring occasionally. Combine onion, turkey, celery, carrots, rice, tarragon and pepper in a slow cooker; stir in broth. Cover and cook on low setting for 6 to 8 hours, or until vegetables and rice are tender. Mix evaporated milk and flour; stir into soup along with peas and sherry, if using. Cover again and cook on low setting for about 20 minutes, or until thickened. Makes 6 servings.

Fluffy dumplings are tasty in any hearty soup.
About 30 minutes before soup is done, mix up
2 cups biscuit baking mix with 3/4 cup milk. Drop by
tablespoonfuls onto simmering soup. Cover and cook
on high setting for 20 to 25 minutes...done!

Chilis, Chowders, Soups & Stews

◆ Supper in a soup bowl ◆

Chicken Stew Over Biscuits

Debi Piper
Vicksburg, MI

One of my family's favorites...my husband and kids always come back for seconds! Very warm and comforting.

2 c. water
3/4 c. white wine or
   chicken broth
2 .87-oz. pkgs. chicken gravy
   mix
2 cloves garlic, minced
1 T. fresh parsley, minced
1 to 2 t. chicken bouillon
   granules
1/2 t. pepper

5 carrots, peeled and cut into
   1-inch pieces
1 onion, cut into 8 wedges
4 skinless, boneless chicken
   breasts, cut into bite-size
   pieces
3 T. all-purpose flour
1/3 c. cold water
16.3-oz. tube refrigerated large
   buttermilk biscuits, baked

Combine first 7 ingredients in a slow cooker; mix until blended. Add carrots, onion and chicken; cover and cook on low setting for 7 to 8 hours. In a small bowl, stir together flour and cold water until smooth; gradually stir into slow cooker. Increase setting to high; cover and cook for one hour. Place biscuits in soup bowls; top with stew. Makes 4 to 6 servings.

Put on a savory stew to cook in your slow cooker, then enjoy winter fun with your family. After a snow hike or ice skating, come home to a hot, delicious dinner waiting...what could be cozier?

Collins' Best Lentil Soup

Michelle Collins
San Diego, CA

This recipe reminds me of a very good friend of mine...he used to make a lentil & sausage soup that I adored.

1 c. dried lentils
1 lb. turkey Kielbasa, sliced
   1/2-inch thick
1 c. onion, chopped
1 c. celery, chopped
1 c. carrots, peeled and chopped

1 c. redskin potato, diced
2 T. fresh flat-leaf parsley,
   chopped
6 c. beef broth
1/2 t. pepper
1/8 t. nutmeg

Combine all ingredients in a slow cooker. Cover and cook on low setting for 6 to 8 hours. Stir before serving. Makes 8 servings.

Split Pea Soup

Penny McShane
Lombard, IL

Choose either green or yellow split peas as you like.

16-oz. pkg. dried split peas
1 c. onion, chopped
1/2 c. celery, chopped
1/2 c. carrots, peeled and sliced
3 cubes chicken bouillon

1 bay leaf
1 t. salt
1/4 t. pepper
1-1/2 c. cooked ham, diced

Soak peas in water overnight; drain and rinse. Combine peas and remaining ingredients except ham in a slow cooker; cover with water. Cover and cook on low setting for 8 to 10 hours, until soup is thick. Add ham during the last hour; discard bay leaf before serving. Makes 4 to 6 servings.

Refrigerate slow-cooked foods or leftovers within
2 hours of turning off the slow cooker.

Chilis, Chowders, Soups & Stews
◈ Supper in a soup bowl ◈

Grandma's Pork Chop Stew

Tara Skillman
Pipersville, PA

Simply delicious!

6 thick boneless pork chops,
  cubed
1 onion, diced
2 T. olive oil
6 to 8 potatoes, peeled
  and cubed

4 stalks celery, chopped
1/2 to 1 c. applesauce
1/2 c. tomato paste
1 t. dried thyme
salt and pepper to taste

In a skillet over medium heat, sauté pork chops and onion in oil; drain. Arrange chops and onion in a slow cooker; top with remaining ingredients. Cover and cook on low setting for at least 3 hours, until chops and potatoes are tender; tastes even better after 8 hours. Makes 6 servings.

Pease porridge hot,
Pease porridge cold,
Pease porridge in the pot
Nine days old.
-Old nursery rhyme

French Onion Soup

Jennifer Knouse
New Oxford, PA

If you're a cheese lover, top each crock of soup with a slice of
Gruyère and broil briefly, until melted and bubbly.

4 c. beef broth
3 c. yellow onion, thinly sliced
1/4 c. butter
1-1/2 t. salt
1/4 c. sugar
2 T. all-purpose flour

Optional: 1/4 c. dry vermouth
  or sherry
1 c. grated Parmesan cheese
8 slices French bread
Optional: additional grated
  Parmesan cheese

Pour broth into a slow cooker set on high; cover and set aside to
warm. In a skillet over medium heat, cook onion slowly in butter
until tender; cover and cook about 15 minutes. Add salt, sugar, flour
and vermouth or sherry, if using. Stir well; add to broth in slow cooker.
Cover and cook on high setting for 3 hours, or reduce heat to low
setting and cook for 6 to 8 hours. At serving time, stir in cheese. Toast
bread in the oven or under a broiler; place bread in soup crocks. Ladle
soup over bread; sprinkle with additional cheese, if desired. Serves 8.

Need to add a little zing to a soup or stew? Just add
a splash of Worcestershire sauce, lemon juice
or flavored vinegar.

Chilis, Chowders, Soups & Stews
◆ Supper in a soup bowl ◆

Beef Barley Soup

Lynne McKaige
Savage, MN

Delicious and satisfying! I like to use a heaping tablespoon of beef soup base instead of bouillon for a much richer beef flavor.

2 c. carrots, peeled and
   thinly sliced
1 c. celery, thinly sliced
3/4 c. green pepper, diced
1 c. onion, diced
1 lb. stew beef, cubed
1/2 c. pearl barley, uncooked

1/4 c. fresh parsley, chopped
3 cubes beef bouillon
2 T. catsup
1 t. salt
3/4 t. dried basil
5 c. water

Layer vegetables, beef and barley in a slow cooker; add seasonings. Pour water over all; do not stir. Cover and cook on low setting for 9 to 11 hours. Makes 4 to 6 servings.

A collection of coffee mugs is fun for serving soup!
Pick up one-of-a-kind novelty or souvenir mugs for
a song at yard sales.

Corny Bacon Chowder

Elizabeth Cisneros
Chino Hills, CA

Tastes even better the day after.

2 T. butter
6 slices bacon, chopped
1/2 red onion, minced
2 T. all-purpose flour
1/4 t. salt
1/4 t. pepper
1/8 t. cayenne pepper

1 c. milk
28-oz. can creamed corn
14-oz. can corn
1/2 red pepper, chopped
1/2 green pepper, chopped
1/2 t. dried parsley

Melt butter in a skillet over medium heat. Add bacon and onion; sauté until bacon is crisp. Add flour, salt, pepper and cayenne pepper to skillet; mix thoroughly. Add milk; cook and stir until thickened. Transfer to a slow cooker; add remaining ingredients. Cover and cook on low setting for 2 to 4 hours. Serves 4 to 6.

When freezing soup, leave a little headspace at
the top...it needs room to expand as it freezes.

Chilis, Chowders, Soups & Stews
◈ Supper in a soup bowl ◈

Finnish Sweet Potato Soup

Sherry Saarinen
Hancock, MI

Sweet potatoes grow abundantly here in the Upper Peninsula
of Michigan. I've found a lot of uses for them, but none is
as tasty as this soup!

3 sweet potatoes, peeled
    and sliced
2 c. chicken broth
1-1/2 c. light cream or
    half-and-half

1 t. sugar
1/8 t. ground cloves
1/8 t. nutmeg
salt to taste
Optional: sour cream, nutmeg

Put sweet potatoes and broth in a slow cooker. Cover and cook on high setting for 2 to 3 hours, until potatoes are tender. Purée in a blender or food processor. Return puréed potatoes to slow cooker; add remaining ingredients. Cover and cook on high setting for an additional one to 2 hours. Serve hot or chilled with a dollop of sour cream and a sprinkle of nutmeg, if desired. Makes about 4 servings.

Homemade croutons add a special touch to soup.
Cut shapes from day-old bread using mini cookie
cutters. Spread with a little softened butter, sprinkle
with garlic powder and bake at 350 degrees for just
a few minutes, until crisp.

Down-on-the-Bayou Gumbo

Sue Neely
Greenville, IL

You can't help but smile with a bowl of gumbo in front of you!

3 T. all-purpose flour
3 T. oil
3 c. chicken broth
1/2 lb. smoked sausage,
   sliced 1/2-inch thick
2 c. frozen okra
14-1/2 oz. can diced tomatoes
1 onion, chopped

1 green pepper, chopped
3 cloves garlic, minced
1/4 t. cayenne pepper
3/4 lb. cooked medium shrimp,
   tails removed
1-1/2 c. long-cooking rice,
   cooked

Stir together flour and oil in a small saucepan over medium heat. Cook, stirring constantly, for 5 minutes. Reduce heat and cook, stirring constantly, for about 10 minutes, or until mixture turns reddish brown. Pour broth into a slow cooker; stir in flour mixture. Add remaining ingredients except shrimp and rice. Cover and cook on low setting for 7 to 9 hours. Shortly before serving, add shrimp to slow cooker; mix well. Cover and cook on low setting for about 20 minutes. Ladle gumbo over cooked rice in soup bowls. Makes 6 servings.

Keep a container in the freezer for leftover veggies, then make a big pot of vegetable soup. Thaw and place in a slow cooker. Add water to cover, seasonings and a can of tomato sauce. Cover and cook on low all day...delicious!

Chilis, Chowders, Soups & Stews

◆ Supper in a soup bowl ◆

Pig-in-a-Poke Ham Soup

Sonia Hawkins
Amarillo, TX

A tasty use for the bone left over from a holiday ham! Or use a smoked ham hock at the butcher's counter.

4 14-1/2 oz. cans green beans
1 meaty ham bone
4 potatoes, peeled and quartered

1 onion, sliced
pepper to taste

In a slow cooker, combine undrained green beans and remaining ingredients. Cover and cook on high setting for one hour. Reduce to low setting; cover and cook for 6 to 7 hours, until the meat falls off the bone. Remove ham bone; dice meat and return to slow cooker. Makes 10 servings.

Prefer not to leave the slow cooker on while you're away? Simple...put it to work overnight!
In the morning, refrigerate food in a fridge container...reheat at suppertime.

Fisherman's Wharf Stew

Marlene Strobel
Perry Hall, MD

Vary this savory stew by adding other seafood like
red snapper and crabmeat.

2 T. olive oil
1 c. leek, sliced
2 cloves garlic, finely chopped
1 c. baby carrots, thinly sliced
6 roma tomatoes, quartered
    and sliced
1/2 c. green pepper, chopped
1/2 t. fennel seed
1 bay leaf
8-oz. bottle clam juice

1 c. dry white wine or water
1 lb. cod, sliced 1-inch thick
    and cubed
1/2 lb. medium shrimp, peeled
    and cleaned
1 t. sugar
1 t. dried basil
1/2 t. salt
1/4 t. hot pepper sauce
2 T. fresh parsley, chopped

Mix oil, leek and garlic in a slow cooker. Add vegetables, fennel seed,
bay leaf, clam juice and wine or water; stir. Cover and cook on low
setting for 8 to 9 hours, until vegetables are tender. About 20 minutes
before serving, gently stir in remaining ingredients except parsley.
Cover and cook on high setting for 15 to 20 minutes, until fish flakes
easily with a fork. Discard bay leaf; stir in parsley. Makes 6 servings.

Crunchy bread sticks are tasty
soup dippers! Stand them up in a
tall, wide flower vase...they'll take
up little space on a soup buffet.

Chilis, Chowders, Soups & Stews
◆ Supper in a soup bowl ◆

New England Clam Chowder
Virginia Watson
Scranton, PA

Once you taste this, you'll never go back to canned chowder!

1/2 c. butter, melted
2 T. onion powder
2 t. dried thyme
2 stalks celery, chopped
46-oz. can clam juice
2 cubes chicken bouillon
2 bay leaves

3 16-oz. cans whole potatoes,
   drained and diced
3 10-oz. cans whole baby clams
2 c. light cream
2 c. milk
salt and pepper to taste

In a 7-quart slow cooker, stir together butter, onion powder, thyme and celery; cook on high setting for 30 minutes. Add clam juice, bouillon, bay leaves and potatoes. Cover and continue cooking on high setting for 2 hours. Add clams and their juice; turn setting to low and cook for an additional 2 hours. Stir in cream and milk; cook for an additional one hour, or until heated through. Before serving, discard bay leaves; add salt and pepper to taste. Makes 6 servings.

Arrange seashells and beach glass from your last vacation on a cake stand. Tuck in some tea lights too...a sweet reminder of happy family times!

Mixed-Up Stew

John Zahn
Hermansville, MI

Chicken and beef together...it's surprisingly tasty!

1/4 c. red steak sauce
1/2 c. hot water
2 cubes chicken bouillon
1 t. sugar
1 t. salt
1/2 t. pepper
2 to 3 lbs. boneless, skinless
   chicken thighs

1 lb. stew beef, cut into
   1-1/2 inch cubes
1 onion, chopped
2 potatoes, peeled and cubed
2 carrots, peeled and thinly
   sliced
16-oz. can stewed tomatoes
1/4 c. all-purpose flour

Combine steak sauce, water, bouillon, sugar, salt and pepper in a slow cooker; stir well. Add remaining ingredients except flour; mix carefully. Cover and cook on low setting for 7 to 10 hours, or on high setting for 4 hours. Make a smooth paste of flour and 1/4 cup of liquid from stew; stir into slow cooker. Cover and cook on high setting until thickened. Makes 6 to 8 servings.

Serve soup in hearty bread bowls...simply hollow out
the centers of round loaves of crusty bread, leaving
the bottom crust.

Chilis, Chowders, Soups & Stews
◆ Supper in a soup bowl ◆

Spicy Beef Stew

Angel Webber
Delaware, OH

A zingy twist on good old beef stew!

1 lb. stew beef, cubed
1 to 2 T. oil
6 potatoes, peeled and diced
1/2 lb. baby carrots
4-oz. jar sliced mushrooms,
   drained

3 c. water
10-3/4 oz. can southwestern
   tomato soup
1/4 c. beef bouillon granules
1/2 t. garlic powder

Brown beef in oil; drain. Combine with remaining ingredients in
a slow cooker. Cover and cook on high for 6 hours. Serves 4 to 6.

Gail's Stuffed Green Pepper Soup

Gail Hickok
Akron, OH

This recipe is a big winner in our house...my husband LOVES it!

1 lb. ground beef, browned
   and drained
2 10-3/4 oz. cans tomato soup
2 8-oz. cans diced tomatoes
2 green peppers, chopped
1 onion, chopped

1 T. Italian seasoning
5.6-oz. pkg. Spanish rice
   mix, uncooked
Garnish: grated Parmesan
   cheese

Combine all ingredients except rice mix and Parmesan cheese in a
slow cooker. Cover and cook on low setting for 3 to 4 hours, until
peppers and onion are soft. Prepare rice mix as package directs; stir
into soup. Cover again and cook on low setting for an additional hour.
Serve with Parmesan cheese sprinkled on top. Makes 4 servings.

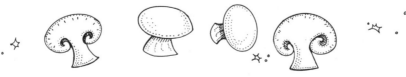

Mamma Mia Italian Stew

Connie Bryant
Topeka, KS

Chock-full of flavorful summer produce.

1 lb. ground hot Italian sausage,
   browned and drained
1 eggplant, peeled and cubed
1-1/2 c. green beans, sliced
2 green peppers, sliced
1 to 2 potatoes, peeled and
   cubed
1 zucchini, cubed

1 yellow squash, cubed
1 c. onion, thinly sliced
15-oz. can Italian-style tomato
   sauce
1/4 c. olive oil
2 t. garlic, minced
1 t. salt

Combine all ingredients in a slow cooker; mix well. Cover and
cook on low setting for 8 hours, or on high setting for 4 hours.
Makes 8 to 10 servings.

Invite friends to a fireside soup supper on a chilly evening!
Place comfy cushions on the floor to sit on and bring
the crock of soup right into the family room.

Chilis, Chowders, Soups & Stews

Italian Meatball Soup

Alice Hardin
Antioch, CA

Sprinkle servings with freshly grated Parmesan cheese.

16-oz. pkg. frozen Italian-style
  meatballs
2 14-oz. cans beef broth
2 14-1/2 oz. cans diced
  tomatoes with Italian herbs

1 c. potato, peeled and chopped
1/2 c. onion, chopped
1/4 t. garlic pepper
16-oz. pkg. frozen mixed
  vegetables

In a slow cooker, mix frozen meatballs with all ingredients except
frozen mixed vegetables. Cover and cook on low setting for 9 to
11 hours. Stir in frozen mixed vegetables. Increase setting to high;
cover and cook for one additional hour, or until vegetables are tender.
Makes 4 to 6 servings.

To skim fat from a pot of soup, lay a slice of bread
on top for just a few minutes.

Tex-Mex Bean Soup

Angela Murphy
Tempe, AZ

Cornmeal dumplings are a delightful homemade touch.

15-1/2 oz. can kidney beans,
   drained and rinsed
15-1/2 oz. can black beans,
   drained and rinsed
14-1/2 oz. can Mexican-style
   stewed tomatoes
10-oz. pkg. frozen corn, thawed

4-oz. can chopped green chiles
1 c. carrots, peeled and sliced
1 c. onion, chopped
2 cloves garlic, minced
3 c. water
2 T. chicken bouillon granules
1 to 2 t. chili powder

Mix all ingredients in a slow cooker. Cover and cook on low setting
for 10 to 12 hours, or on high setting for 4 to 5 hours. Turn slow
cooker to high setting; drop dumpling batter into soup by rounded
teaspoonfuls. Cover and cook for 30 minutes without lifting lid.
Makes 4 to 6 servings.

Cornmeal Dumplings:

1/3 c. all-purpose flour
1/4 c. cornmeal
1 t. baking powder
1/8 t. salt

1/8 t. pepper
1 egg white, beaten
2 T. milk
1 T. oil

Mix flour, cornmeal, baking powder, salt and pepper; set aside.
Mix egg white, milk and oil; stir into flour mixture. Stir with a fork
until just combined.

Good manners: The noise you don't make
when you're eating soup.

-Bennett Cerf

Chilis, Chowders, Soups & Stews
◆ Supper in a soup bowl ◆

Santa Fe Corn & Bean Soup

Athena Colegrove
Big Springs, TX

Garnish with shredded Monterey Jack cheese...it's good enough for company!

1 lb. ground beef
1/2 onion, diced
2 10-oz. can tomatoes with
  chiles
2 c. water
16-oz. can kidney beans
16-oz. can pinto beans

16-oz. can black beans
11-oz. can corn
1-oz. pkg. ranch salad dressing
  mix
1-1/4 oz. pkg. taco seasoning
  mix

Brown beef and onion together in a skillet; drain. Transfer to a slow cooker; mix in remaining ingredients. Cover and cook on low setting for 6 to 8 hours, or on high setting for 3 to 4 hours, until heated through. Serves 6 to 8.

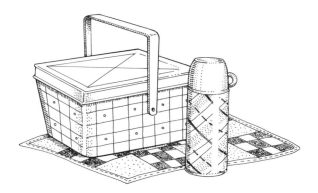

Tote along a vintage thermos filled with hot soup on a cool-weather nature walk...it'll really hit the spot! Before ladling in the soup, prewarm the thermos with hot water for 10 minutes.

Rio Grande Green Pork Chili
Debby Heatwole
Canadian, TX

Makes a wonderful buffet dish served with warm flour tortillas, or spoon over potato-filled burritos...yum!

3 lbs. boneless pork steak,
   cubed
1 clove garlic, minced
3 T. olive oil
1/2 c. all-purpose flour
2 14-1/2 oz. cans beef broth
32-oz. can tomato juice
14-1/2 oz. can crushed tomatoes

7-oz. can diced green chiles
4-oz. can chopped jalapeño
   peppers
1/3 c. dried parsley
1/4 c. lemon juice
2 t. ground cumin
1 t. sugar
1/4 t. ground cloves

In a heavy skillet over medium heat, sauté pork and garlic in oil. Add flour, stirring until thoroughly mixed. Drain; place browned pork in a slow cooker. Add remaining ingredients; cover and cook on low setting for 6 to 8 hours, until pork is tender. Serves 12 to 14.

There's no such thing as too much chili! Top hot dogs and baked potatoes with extra chili...spoon into flour tortillas and sprinkle with shredded cheese for quick burritos.

Sandwiches & More

Dinner on a bun

Hearty Italian Sandwiches

Kristie Rigo
Friedens, PA

Messy but delicious...pass the napkins, please!

1 lb. ground beef
1 lb. ground Italian sausage
1 onion, chopped
1 green pepper, chopped
1 red pepper, chopped
1 t. salt

1 t. pepper
1/2 t. red pepper flakes
3/4 c. Italian salad dressing
12 sandwich rolls, split
12 slices provolone cheese

Brown ground beef and sausage together in a skillet; drain and set aside. Place one-third of onion and peppers in a slow cooker; top with half of meat mixture. Repeat layers with remaining vegetables and meat. Sprinkle with salt, pepper and red pepper flakes; pour salad dressing over top. Cover and cook on low setting for 6 hours. Serve on rolls, topped with cheese. Makes 12 sandwiches.

Feeding a crowd is a breeze with a slow cooker. Fill it up with cooked sausages, hot dogs or meatballs, set out bakery-fresh rolls, chips and coleslaw...and you're ready to just let guests help themselves!

❖ Sandwiches & More ❖
Dinner on a bun

Italian Meatball Subs

Clydia Mims
Effingham, SC

*This recipe is so good! I like to make a double batch and freeze half
for another meal...the meatballs are good over pasta too!*

1 lb. ground beef
1 c. Italian-seasoned
   bread crumbs
1/2 c. grated Parmesan cheese
1 T. fresh parsley, minced
1 clove garlic, minced

1/2 c. milk
1 egg
1-1/2 t. salt
1/2 t. pepper
8 hot dog buns, split

Combine all ingredients except buns in a large bowl; mix well. Form
into 2-inch balls and place in a slow cooker; pour sauce over top.
Cover and cook on low setting for 8 to 10 hours, or on high setting
for 4 to 6 hours. To serve, place 3 to 4 meatballs on a bun; top with
sauce from slow cooker. Makes 8 sandwiches.

Sauce:

28-oz. can tomato purée
28-oz. can Italian-style crushed
   tomatoes
1/2 c. grated Parmesan cheese

2 1-1/2 oz. pkgs. spaghetti
   sauce mix
salt and pepper to taste

Mix all ingredients in a saucepan; bring to a boil. Reduce heat and
simmer until blended.

Allow a little extra time when slow-cooking in
summertime...high humidity can cause food
to take longer to finish cooking.

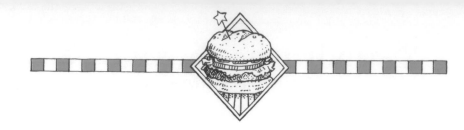

Apple Pork BBQ

Lynn Matava
Hebron, MD

A real crowd pleaser!

5 to 7-lb. pork picnic roast
5 cloves garlic
1 sweet onion, chopped
2 c. hot & spicy barbecue sauce

1-1/2 c. applesauce
1 t. cinnamon
salt and pepper to taste
10 to 12 kaiser rolls, split

Cut roast into 2 or 3 pieces to fit into slow cooker, if necessary. Top with whole garlic cloves and chopped onion; add water to cover roast. Cover and cook for 10 to 14 hours, or overnight. When pork is tender and easily shredded, drain and discard cooking liquid. Break roast apart in slow cooker and shred, removing any bones; mash and blend in garlic. Combine barbecue sauce and applesauce; toss with pulled pork to coat thoroughly. Sprinkle with cinnamon, salt and pepper. Cover and cook on low setting until warmed through. Serve pork spooned into rolls. Makes 10 to 12 sandwiches.

Pack up sandwiches in box lunches for old-fashioned fun!
Decorate shoe boxes with wrapping paper and tie with a
big ribbon bow...tuck in a bag of chips and a cookie.

Slow-Cooker Breakfast Casserole, page 21

Bacon-Horseradish Dip, page 174

Heartland Barbecued Beef, page 127

Slow-Cooker Sweet Potato Chili, page 25

Creamy Tomato Soup, page 103

Pepperoncini Italian Beef Roast, page 144

Anne's Chicken Burritos,, page 141

Mom's Slow-Cooker Mini Reubens, page 175

Festive Apples & Squash, page 147

Joan's Chicken Stuffing Casserole, page 60

Hot Buffalo Dip, page 180

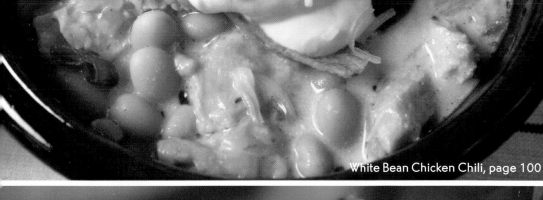

White Bean Chicken Chili, page 100

The Best Pot Roast Ever,
page 44

Apple-Stuffed Turkey Breast, page 48

Autumn Apple-Pecan Dressing, page 168

Santa Fe Turkey Stew, page 15

Famous Broccoli Casserole, page 148

Mexican Albondigas Soup, page 87

Spaghetti Sauce for a Crowd, page 11

Double-Berry Cobbler, page 199

Apple Brown Betty, page 211

Lemon-Poppy Seed Cake, page 213

❖ Sandwiches & More ❖
Dinner on a bun

Heartland Barbecued Beef

Sharon Crider
Junction City, KS

So much flavor for so little effort.

2-lb. beef chuck roast, cut
    crosswise into 1/4-inch
    slices
1/2 c. onion, chopped
2 cloves garlic, minced
2 c. catsup

1/4 c. brown sugar, packed
1/4 c. Worcestershire sauce
1 t. mustard
1/2 t. salt
1/4 t. pepper
6 to 8 onion buns, split

Combine all ingredients except buns in a slow cooker; mix well.
Cover and cook on low setting for 6 to 8 hours, stirring occasionally,
until meat is tender. Serve on buns. Makes 6 to 8 sandwiches.

Bar-B-Q Steak Sandwiches

Lisa Sanders
Shoals, IN

A great party recipe! Roll up leftovers in tortillas for a fast lunch.

3 lbs. boneless beef round steak,
    cut into several large pieces
2 onions, chopped
3/4 c. celery, thinly sliced
1/2 c. catsup
1/2 to 3/4 c. water
1/3 c. lemon juice
1/3 c. Worcestershire sauce
3 T. brown sugar, packed

3 T. cider vinegar
2 t. mustard
1 t. chili powder
1/2 t. hot pepper sauce
1/2 t. paprika
2 t. salt
1 t. pepper
12 to 14 hamburger buns, split

Place meat, onions and celery in a slow cooker; set aside. Combine
remaining ingredients except buns in a bowl. Stir and pour over meat.
Cover and cook for 6 to 8 hours, until meat is tender. Remove meat
and cool slightly; shred with a fork and return to sauce in slow cooker.
Heat through and serve on buns. Makes 12 to 14 sandwiches.

Mexicali Beef Soft Tacos

Kathy Lowe
Orem, UT

*Two meals in one! I make tacos the first night, then another night
I warm the remaining meat with barbecue sauce for sandwiches.*

1/2 to 1 c. water
4 to 5-lb. beef chuck roast
1/2 red onion, chopped
3 cloves garlic
1/4 c. oil
1 T. red pepper flakes
2 t. ground cumin

2 t. dried oregano
1 t. pepper
10 to 12 10-inch flour tortillas,
   warmed
Garnish: lettuce, chopped onion,
   chopped tomatoes, sour
   cream, salsa

Pour water into a slow cooker; add roast and set aside. Combine
onion, garlic, oil and seasonings in a blender. Blend until mixed; pour
over roast. Cover and cook on high setting for about 7 hours, until
roast is very tender. Shred roast with 2 forks; return to slow cooker.
Cover and cook on low setting for an additional hour. Fill tortillas with
beef mixture; add toppings as desired. Makes 10 to 12 servings.

A basket of warmed flour tortillas is a must-have
with fajitas and burritos. Simply wrap tortillas
in aluminum foil and pop into a 250-degree
oven for about 15 minutes...easy!

Zippy Shredded Pork

Kathleen Souza
Acushnet, MA

I like to add some canned chipotle peppers in adobo sauce...they give a really good smokey flavor.

2 to 3-lb. boneless pork loin
   roast
salt and pepper to taste
16-oz. jar salsa

Optional: hot pepper sauce,
   chopped green chiles
6 hard rolls, split

Place roast in a slow cooker; sprinkle with salt and pepper. Pour salsa over roast; add hot sauce or chiles for extra heat, if desired. Cover and cook on low setting for 8 to 10 hours, or until meat shreds easily. Stir meat to shred completely and serve on rolls. Makes 6 servings.

Juicy BBQ sandwiches are best served on a vintage-style oilcloth...saucy spills wipe right up! Look for one with a colorful design of fruit or flowers.

Savory Chicken Sandwiches

Jodi Griggs
Richmond, KY

*We've made these sandwiches lots of times when we had family &
friends coming for the day...it's so easy to make ahead.
Everyone always asks for seconds or thirds!*

4 boneless, skinless chicken
   breasts
1-1/2 oz. pkg. onion soup mix
1/4 t. garlic salt
1/4 c. Italian salad dressing

1/4 c. water
4 sandwich buns, split
Garnish: lettuce, sliced cheese,
   sour cream or ranch
   salad dressing

Place chicken in a slow cooker; sprinkle with soup mix and garlic salt.
Pour dressing and water over chicken. Cover and cook on low setting
for 8 to 9 hours. Remove chicken and shred with 2 forks; return to
slow cooker. Serve with a slotted spoon on buns; garnish as desired.
Makes 4 sandwiches.

Keep a basket packed with paper plates, napkins and cups.
You'll be ready for a family picnic at a moment's
notice...just grab dinner in the slow cooker and go!

❖ Sandwiches & More ❖
Dinner on a bun

Yummy Ham Sandwiches *Beth Cavanaugh Brown*
Columbus, OH

Welcome at any carry-in dinner.

6-lb. bone-in ham
8-oz. jar mustard

16-oz. pkg. brown sugar
24 dinner rolls, split

Place ham in a slow cooker; cover with water. Cover and cook on low
setting for 8 to 10 hours, until ham is very tender. Drain and let cool.
Shred ham and return to slow cooker; stir in mustard and brown
sugar. Cover and cook on low just until heated through. Serve on rolls.
Makes 24 sandwiches.

Ham-Stuffed French Rolls *Barbara Fiecoat*
Galena, OH

Serve the hot rolls right from the slow cooker.

2 c. cooked ham, finely chopped
1/2 c. Cheddar cheese, diced
1/3 c. mayonnaise
2 T. green onion, minced
1 t. mustard
1 t. sweet pickle relish

Optional: 2 eggs, hard-boiled,
   peeled and chopped
Optional: 2 T. black olives,
   chopped
6 large or 8 small French rolls

Combine all ingredients except rolls; set aside. Cut tops or one end
off rolls; scoop out most of soft centers. Fill rolls with ham mixture;
replace tops or ends of rolls. Place filled rolls in a slow cooker. Cover
and cook on low setting for 2 to 3 hours. Makes 6 to 8 sandwiches.

Pita halves are perfect
for slow-cooker sandwich
fillings...extra easy for little
hands to hold without spills!

Made-Rights

Linda Bair
Jeffersonville, OH

A local tradition! I like to fix plenty of the ground beef so I can use leftovers for taco salads, chili and casseroles.

4 lbs. ground beef
3 c. water
1 c. cola

1/2 c. mustard
1 c. catsup
20 to 24 sandwich buns, split

Combine ground beef, water and cola in a slow cooker. With a potato masher, break the beef apart. Cover and cook on low setting for 8 to 10 hours. After meat is thoroughly cooked, mash again; drain well. Stir in mustard and catsup; serve on sandwich buns. Makes 20 to 24 sandwiches.

Warm sandwich buns for a crowd...easy! Fill a roaster with buns, cover with heavy-duty aluminum foil and cut several slits in the foil. Top with several dampened paper towels and tightly cover with more foil. Place in a 250-degree oven for 20 minutes. Rolls will be hot and steamy.

◈ Sandwiches & More ◈
Dinner on a bun

Saucy Hamburgers

Jennifer Kann
Dayton, OH

Add onion and chili powder to taste if you enjoy a spicier burger.

1-1/2 lbs. ground beef
1 onion, sliced into rings
1 c. catsup
1/2 to 3/4 c. water

2 T. butter, melted
2 T. sugar
salt and pepper to taste
6 hamburger buns, split

Form ground beef into 6 patties. Brown in a skillet over medium heat; drain. Combine remaining ingredients except buns in a slow cooker; stir to blend. Add hamburgers; cover and cook on low setting for 3 to 4 hours. Serve on buns. Makes 6 sandwiches.

Aunt B's Sloppy Joes

Bryna Dunlap
Muskogee, OK

For a quick & easy meal, ladle leftovers over cooked rotini pasta.

3 lbs. ground turkey
1 c. onion, chopped
1 c. green pepper, chopped
2 cloves garlic, chopped
1-1/2 c. catsup
1/2 c. water

1/4 c. mustard
1/4 c. cider vinegar
1/4 c. Worcestershire sauce
1 T. chili powder
10 whole-wheat hamburger
    buns, split

In a skillet over medium heat, cook ground turkey, onion, green pepper and garlic until browned and tender; drain. Combine in a slow cooker with remaining ingredients except buns. Cover and cook on low setting for 6 to 8 hours, or on high setting for 3 to 4 hours. Spoon into buns. Makes about 10 sandwiches.

Creamy Chicken Sandwiches
Darcie Meligan
Mansfield, OH

A Midwestern favorite.

2 13-oz. cans chicken, drained
10-3/4 oz. can cream of
   chicken soup
10-3/4 oz. can cream of
   mushroom soup

1 t. garlic powder
pepper to taste
1 c. potato chips, coarsely
   crushed
8 to 10 buns, split

Mix together chicken and soups; add seasonings and crushed chips. Spoon into a slow cooker; cover and cook on high setting for 4 hours. Serve on buns. Makes 8 to 10.

BBQ Chicken Sandwiches
Tina Dammrich
St. Louis, MO

Just 3 ingredients, but oh-so-tasty!

4-lb. chicken
1-1/2 to 2 c. hickory smoke-
   flavored barbecue sauce

8 to 10 sandwich buns, split

Place chicken in a stockpot. Add water to cover and simmer until tender, about one hour. Remove chicken and cool; pull meat from bones. Place chicken in a slow cooker; cover with barbecue sauce. Cover and cook on high setting for 3 to 5 hours, stirring every 30 minutes. Chicken will shred during stirring. Serve on buns. Makes 8 to 10 sandwiches.

Greek Chicken Pitas

Peggy Pelfrey
Fort Riley, KS

Top with crumbled feta cheese and sliced black olives.

1 onion, diced
3 cloves garlic, minced
1 lb. boneless, skinless chicken
   breasts, cut into strips
1 t. lemon-pepper seasoning
1/2 t. dried oregano
1/4 t. allspice

1/4 c. plain yogurt
1/4 c. sour cream
1/2 c. cucumber, peeled
   and diced
4 rounds pita bread, halved
   and split

Place onion and garlic in a slow cooker; set aside. Sprinkle chicken with seasonings; place in slow cooker. Cover and cook on high setting for 6 hours. Stir together yogurt, sour cream and cucumber in a small bowl; chill. Fill pita halves with chicken and drizzle with yogurt sauce. Makes 4 sandwiches.

Slow-cooker potlucks are perfect for family reunions.
You'll be free to chat, play games and just have a good
time together all day while the slow cookers cook!

Ballpark Hot Dogs

Diana Krol
Nickerson, KS

Mmm...hot dogs cook slowly in their own juices! I've fixed thousands of wieners this way for our baseball concession stand.

16-oz. pkg. hot dogs   Garnish: favorite condiments
10 hot dog buns, split

Place hot dogs in a slow cooker. Cover and cook on low setting for up to 5 hours, or on high setting for 2 hours. Serve in buns, straight from the slow cooker, garnished as desired. Serves 10.

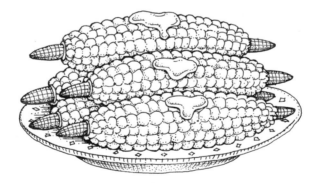

Sweet corn for a crowd! Peel back husks, remove
silk and rewrap husks. Trim ends and stand ears upright
in a deep slow cooker. Cover and cook on high for
45 minutes, reduce to low and cook for
1-1/2 to 2 hours. Mmm...pass the butter!

World's Best Bratwurst

Dee Ann Ice
Delaware, OH

Use either sweet or spicy bratwurst...your choice!

2 lbs. bratwurst
2 T. oil
32-oz. jar spaghetti sauce
1/2 to 3/4 c. barbecue sauce

2 onions, thickly sliced
1 green pepper, sliced
8 to 10 hot dog buns, split
   and toasted

Brown brats in oil in a skillet over medium heat. Place brats and
pan drippings in a slow cooker. Add sauces, onions and pepper; stir
together to combine. Cover and cook on high setting for 3 to 4 hours;
reduce heat to low setting and cook for an additional 4 to 5 hours.
Serve on toasted buns. Makes 8 to 10 sandwiches.

Hollowed-out peppers make garden-fresh servers for
catsup, relish and mustard! Just cut a slice off
the bottom so they'll sit flat.

BBQ Pulled Pork Fajitas

Jackie Valvardi
Haddon Heights, NJ

We like to spice these up with shredded Pepper Jack cheese.

2-1/2 lb. boneless pork loin
   roast, trimmed
1 onion, thinly sliced
2 c. barbecue sauce
3/4 c. chunky salsa
1 T. chili powder
1 t. ground cumin

16-oz. pkg. frozen stir-fry
   peppers and onions
1/2 t. salt
18 8 to 10-inch flour tortillas,
   warmed
Garnish: shredded cheese,
   guacamole, sour cream

Place pork in a slow cooker; top with onion and set aside. Mix sauce, salsa and spices in a bowl; pour over top. Cover and cook on low setting for 8 to 10 hours. Remove pork and place on a cutting board; shred, using 2 forks. Return to slow cooker and mix well; add stir-fry vegetables and salt. Increase setting to high; cover and cook for an additional 30 minutes, until hot and vegetables are tender. With a slotted spoon, fill each warmed tortilla with 1/2 cup pork mixture. Fold one end of tortilla up and one inch over filling; overlap and fold sides over folded end. Fold remaining end down. Serve with garnishes as desired. Makes 18 servings.

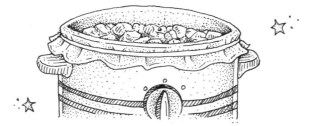

Save time on clean-up. Look for plastic liners made especially for slow cookers or tuck food into a plastic oven roasting bag...simply cook and toss!

Mexican Roll-Ups

Ali Snow
Boston, MA

*Makes a yummy taco salad too! Just layer ingredients over
shredded lettuce in crisp tostada bowls.*

2 lbs. beef flank steak
1-1/4 oz. pkg. taco seasoning
   mix
1 T. butter
1 c. red onion, diced
1 c. green chiles, diced
1 T. cider vinegar

16-oz. can refried beans
12 8-inch flour tortillas, warmed
1-1/2 c. shredded Cheddar
   cheese
2 c. cherry tomatoes, diced
8-oz. container sour cream

Rub flank steak on all sides with taco seasoning; place in a slow
cooker coated with butter. Add onion, chiles and vinegar; cover and
cook on low setting for 9 hours. Remove beef from slow cooker and
shred. Place beef back in slow cooker with cooking juices; stir well.
Heat refried beans and tortillas according to package directions.
Spread one to 2 tablespoons refried beans down the center of each
tortilla. Spoon about 1/3 cup beef mixture over refried beans. Top each
with 2 tablespoons cheese, 2 tablespoons tomato and one tablespoon
sour cream; roll up. Makes 12 servings.

Serve up icy lemonade in
frosted-rim glasses! Chill
tumblers in the fridge. At
serving time, moisten rims
with lemon juice or water
and dip into a dish
of sparkling sugar.

Smokey BBQ Beef Rolls

Carolyn Greenmyer
Stigler, OK

You won't believe how scrumptious this beef is...it tastes like it's right off the smoker!

4 to 6-lb. beef brisket
1 T. onion salt
1 T. celery salt
1 t. garlic salt
coarse pepper to taste

1/4 c. smoke-flavored cooking
    sauce
1/4 c. Worcestershire sauce
16 rolls, split

Rub brisket with salts and pepper; place in slow cooker. Stir sauces together; gently pour over roast. Cover; cook on low setting for 8 to 10 hours. Slice or shred meat; serve on rolls. Makes 16 sandwiches.

French Dip

Debbie DeValk
Springfield, TN

Pour the delicious broth into small cups for dipping.

3-lb. beef chuck roast, trimmed
2 c. water
1/2 c. soy sauce
1 t. dried rosemary
1 t. dried thyme

1 t. garlic powder
1 bay leaf
3 to 4 whole peppercorns
8 French rolls, split

Place roast in a slow cooker; add water, soy sauce and seasonings. Cover and cook on high for 5 to 6 hours. Remove meat from broth; shred with a fork and keep warm. Discard bay leaf; serve sliced beef on rolls. Makes 6 to 8 sandwiches.

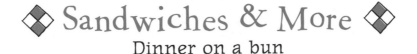
Anne's Chicken Burritos

Jennifer Sievers
Roselle, IL

My friend, Anne, gave me this easy slow-cooker recipe...we love it more and more each time we make it!

6 boneless, skinless chicken
   breasts
15-1/4 oz. can corn, drained
16-oz. can black beans, drained
   and rinsed

16-oz. jar salsa
6 to 8 10-inch flour tortillas
Garnish: shredded Cheddar
   cheese, sour cream, salsa,
   guacamole

Place chicken in a slow cooker; top with corn, beans and salsa. Cover and cook on low setting for 8 to 10 hours, or on high setting for 4 to 6 hours. Shred chicken; stir back into slow cooker. To serve, spoon mixture onto tortillas. Add desired garnishes and roll up. Serves 6 to 8.

Rolls and buns will drip less when filled with juicy slow-cooked meat if they're toasted first.

Fiesta Beef Fajitas

Shelly Livingston
Shamrock, TX

Flavorful skirt steak is traditional in fajitas, but if your butcher doesn't offer it, flank steak is also good.

2 lbs. beef skirt or flank steak
14-1/2 oz. can tomatoes
  with chiles
2 1-1/4 oz. pkgs. fajita
  seasoning mix
1 onion, coarsely chopped

1 green pepper, coarsely
  chopped
8 to 12 10-inch flour tortillas,
  warmed
Garnish: guacamole, sour cream,
  shredded cheese, salsa

Place meat in a slow cooker and set aside. Mix tomatoes with chiles and fajita seasoning together in a bowl; pour over meat. Cover and cook on high setting for 4 hours; reduce to low and cook for an additional 2 hours. Add onion and green pepper; cover and continue cooking on low setting for an additional hour. Shred meat; serve on warmed tortillas with desired garnishes. Makes 4 to 6 servings.

Serve up hot & tasty sandwich fixin's at your next tailgating party...right out of a slow cooker! Plug it into a power inverter that uses your car battery to power appliances.

◆ Sandwiches & More ◆
Dinner on a bun

Slow-Cooked Pork Tacos

Janet Allen
Hauser, ID

Fill crunchy folded corn tortillas for a different taste.

1 onion, chopped
1 green pepper, chopped
1-1/2 lbs. boneless pork
    loin chops
3/4 c. orange juice
juice of 1 lime
1/2 c. fresh cilantro, chopped
1 T. garlic, chopped

1 t. chili powder
salt and pepper to taste
3/4 c. salsa
8 8-inch flour tortillas, warmed
Garnish: lettuce, tomato, sour
    cream, salsa

Place onion and pepper into a slow cooker; add pork. Mix together remaining ingredients except tortillas and garnish; pour over meat. Cover and cook on low setting for 4 to 6 hours, until meat is very tender. Drain excess liquid; shred meat with a fork. Spoon into warmed tortillas and add taco toppings of your choice. Serves 4.

Serve tacos or fajitas in a new way. Layer meat, lettuce and veggies in large clear plastic cups. Top with shredded cheese, chopped avocado and a dollop of sour cream. Provide sturdy plastic forks...guests can stroll and eat!

Pepperoncini Italian Beef Roast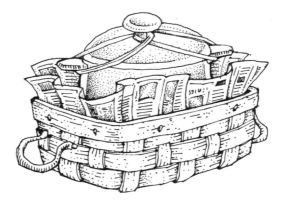

Vickie

These sandwiches are zesty and oh-so easy to fix!

4-lb. beef chuck roast
8-oz. jar pepperoncini peppers,
   drained and juice reserved

1 onion, sliced
2 1-oz. pkgs. au jus mix
8 to 10 hoagie rolls, split

Place roast in a slow cooker; pour reserved pepper juice over top. Cover and cook on low setting for 6 to 8 hours, until very tender. Remove roast and shred with 2 forks; stir back into juice in slow cooker. Add peppers and onion. Blend au jus mix with a little of the juice from slow cooker until dissolved. Pour over meat; add water if needed to cover roast. Cover and cook for an additional hour. Serve beef spooned onto rolls. Makes 8 to 10 sandwiches.

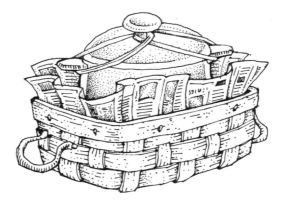

Carry along a slow cooker without spilling...just pull
2 large rubber bands around the knob on the lid
and the handles. Wrap it in newspaper to hold in
the heat...just plug in the slow cooker when you arrive.
Food will stay hot and delicious.

Scrumptious Sides

Tasty side dishes

Harvest Pecan Sweet Potatoes
Nancy Girard
Chesapeake, VA

A delicious addition to a holiday meal...I always get lots of compliments!

2 29-oz. cans sweet potatoes, drained
1/3 c. plus 2 t. butter, melted and divided
2 T. sugar
1/3 c. plus 2 T. brown sugar, packed and divided

1 T. orange juice
2 eggs, beaten
1/2 c. milk
1/3 c. chopped pecans
2 T. all-purpose flour

Mash sweet potatoes in a large bowl; blend in 1/3 cup melted butter, sugar and 2 tablespoons brown sugar. Beat in orange juice, eggs and milk; spoon into a lightly greased slow cooker and set aside. Combine pecans, flour, remaining brown sugar and remaining butter in a small bowl. Spread mixture over sweet potatoes; cover and cook on high setting for 3 to 4 hours. Makes 8 to 10 servings.

Enlist your crockery cooker as a handy holiday helper! If there's a turkey in the oven and dishes simmering on the stove, simply fill up slow cookers with potatoes, dressing and other sides and let 'em cook away on the countertop.

◈ Scrumptious Sides ◈
Tasty side dishes

Festive Apples & Squash
JoAnna Nicoline-Haughey
Berwyn, PA

*I love the aroma of the spices throughout the house
while this is cooking!*

4 lbs. butternut squash
2/3 c. butter, melted
1 c. light brown sugar, packed
1/2 t. salt
3 T. all-purpose flour

1 t. cinnamon
1/2 t. ground ginger
1/2 t. nutmeg
6 Granny Smith apples, peeled,
   cored and sliced

Cut squash in half; remove seeds, peel and cut into 1/2-inch cubes.
Combine butter, brown sugar, salt, flour and spices; mix until crumbly.
Layer half of squash in an oval slow cooker. Top with half of the
apple slices and half of the spice mixture. Repeat layers. Cover and
cook on low setting for 6 hours, or on high setting for 3-1/2 hours.
Serves 6 to 8.

Bring the whole neighborhood together with a progressive
dinner! Start at one end of the street with slow-cooker
appetizers...finish at the other end with dessert.
With crocks of prepared food set on low or warm,
everyone can go from house to house together
without missing any of the fun or food.

Famous Broccoli Casserole

Paul Gaulke
Newark, OH

*This casserole recipe is tried & true...we can't imagine
a **Gooseberry Patch** potluck without it!*

16-oz. pkg. frozen broccoli
10-oz. pkg. frozen broccoli
2 10-3/4 oz. cans cream of
   chicken soup

16-oz. pkg. pasteurized process
   cheese spread, cubed
2 6.9-oz. pkgs. chicken-flavored
   rice vermicelli mix, prepared

Cook and drain broccoli; place in a slow cooker. Add soup and cheese; mix well. Stir in prepared rice vermicelli mix. Cover and cook on low setting for 3 to 4 hours, until hot and bubbly. Makes 32 servings.

Need more space at the dining table? Here's a quick
solution...simply lay a door across 2 sawhorses.
Cover with a tablecloth and no one
will know the difference!

Spoon Bread Florentine

Jo Ann

Deliciously different and so simple to make.

10-oz. pkg. frozen chopped
    spinach, thawed and drained
6 green onions, sliced
1 red pepper, chopped
5-1/2 oz. pkg. cornbread mix

4 eggs, beaten
1/2 c. butter, melted
1 c. cottage cheese
1-1/4 t. seasoned salt

Combine all ingredients in a large bowl; mix well. Spoon into a lightly greased slow cooker. Cover, with lid slightly ajar to allow moisture to escape. Cook on low setting for 3 to 4 hours, or on high setting for 1-3/4 to 2 hours, until edges are golden and a knife tip inserted in center tests clean. Makes 8 servings.

Keep slow-cooked food hot for carry-ins...wrap
the crock in several layers of newspaper, then set in
an insulated cooler. Food will stay warm for
up to 2 hours.

Savory Southern-Style Greens

Staci Meyers
Cocoa, FL

Be sure to save the flavorful "pot liquor" or cooking broth...use it instead of water for cooking rice.

2 smoked ham hocks
6 c. water, divided
3 to 4 cubes ham bouillon
2 T. sugar
2 T. vinegar brine from a jar of
   sliced jalapeño peppers

seasoned salt and pepper
   to taste
1 bunch collard greens,
   trimmed and sliced into
   1/2-inch strips
cooked rice

Combine ham hocks and 2 cups water in a stockpot; bring to a boil. Reduce heat and simmer for 15 to 30 minutes. Stir in remaining water and other ingredients except greens and rice. Transfer ham hocks and greens to a slow cooker; pour hot broth over top. Cover and cook on low setting for 8 hours or overnight, until greens are tender but not mushy, adding more water as necessary to keep pot at least half full of liquid. Remove ham hocks; dice meat and return to slow cooker. For best flavor, cool and refrigerate, reheating next day at serving time. Serve over cooked rice. Makes 6 to 8 servings.

Set a tall pillar candle in the center of a seasonal wreath...a clever centerpiece in a jiffy!

❖ Scrumptious Sides ❖
Tasty side dishes

Hearty Red Beans & Rice
Tyson Ann Trecannelli
Fishing Creek, MD

Real down-home goodness!

16-oz. pkg. dried kidney beans
2 T. oil
1 onion, chopped
3 stalks celery, chopped
1 green pepper, chopped
2 cloves garlic, minced
3 c. water

2-2/3 c. beef broth
1/2 t. red pepper flakes
1 meaty ham bone or ham hock
1 t. salt
cooked rice
Garnish: chopped green onions,
    crisply cooked bacon

Soak beans overnight in water to cover; drain and set aside. In a large skillet, heat oil over medium-high heat. Add onion, celery, pepper and garlic; sauté until onion is translucent, 5 to 6 minutes. Place in a slow cooker along with drained beans, water, broth and red pepper flakes. Add ham bone and push down into mixture. Cover and cook on low setting until beans are very tender, 9 to 10 hours. Remove ham bone; dice meat and return to slow cooker. Stir in salt. Serve beans spooned over hot cooked rice in bowls. Garnish with green onions and bacon. Serves 6 to 8.

Instead of soaking, dried beans can be slow-cooked
overnight on low. Cover with water and add a teaspoon
of baking soda. In the morning, just drain
and proceed with the recipe.

Macaroni & 4 Cheeses

Ursula Juarez-Wall
Dumfries, VA

*As a busy military wife and mother of 4, I often turned to
my slow cooker to help with dinners on hectic days.
This is an all-time favorite recipe.*

3 c. cooked elbow macaroni
1 T. margarine, melted
2 c. evaporated milk
3/4 c. shredded Cheddar cheese
3/4 c. shredded Monterey Jack
    or Colby Jack cheese
3/4 c. shredded Gruyère or
    Swiss cheese

3/4 c. pasteurized process
    cheese spread, cubed
1/4 c. onion, finely chopped
1/4 c. green pepper, finely
    chopped
1 t. seasoned salt
1/4 t. pepper

Combine macaroni and margarine in a lightly greased slow cooker.
Add remaining ingredients; mix well. Cover and cook on high setting
for 2 to 3 hours, stirring once or twice. Serves 4 to 6.

Wrap and freeze small amounts of leftover cheeses.
They may become crumbly when thawed, but will
still be delicious in slow-cooker casseroles.

◆ Scrumptious Sides ◆
Tasty side dishes

Cheesy Crock Potatoes

Daphne Mann
Waukesha, WI

A real winner...you may want to make a double batch!

24-oz. pkg. frozen shredded
   hashbrowns, thawed
10-3/4 oz. can cream of
   potato soup
16-oz. container ranch dip

1 to 2 c. shredded Cheddar
   cheese
salt, pepper and garlic powder
   to taste
6-oz. can French fried onions

Combine hashbrowns, soup, dip, cheese and seasonings in a slow
cooker; heat on low setting for 4 to 6 hours, stirring once. Sprinkle
with onions before serving. Serves 4 to 6.

Potatoes Dijonnaise

Dawn Dhooghe
Concord, NC

The house smells heavenly while this is cooking!

1/3 c. Dijon mustard
1/2 c. olive oil
1/3 c. red wine vinegar

salt and pepper to taste
6 potatoes, cubed
1 onion, chopped

Blend mustard, oil and vinegar in a medium bowl; add salt and pepper
to taste. Add potatoes and onion, stirring to coat. Transfer to a slow
cooker; cover and cook on low setting for 8 to 10 hours, or until
potatoes are tender. Makes 4 to 5 servings.

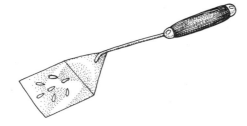

Put new, large terra cotta
saucers to use as picnic
serving bowls...just line
with wax paper.

Asparagus & Cheese Hot Dish
Dianna Likens
Powell, OH

Family members will gladly eat their veggies!

1-1/2 to 2 lbs. asparagus,
   trimmed and sliced
1 egg, beaten
1 c. saltine cracker crumbs
10-3/4 oz. can cream of
   asparagus soup

10-3/4 oz. can cream of
   chicken soup
1/4 lb. pasteurized process
   cheese spread, cubed
2/3 c. slivered almonds

Combine all ingredients in a slow cooker; mix well. Cover and cook on high setting for 3 to 3-1/2 hours, until asparagus is tender. Makes 4 to 6 servings.

Cheddar Cheese Strata
Tracy McIntire
Delaware, OH

Makes a delightful brunch dish.

8 slices bread, crusts trimmed
8-oz. pkg. shredded sharp
   Cheddar cheese
4 eggs
1 c. light cream

1 c. evaporated milk
1 T. dried parsley
1/4 t. salt
Garnish: paprika

Tear bread into bite-size pieces. Alternate layers of bread and cheese in a slow cooker; set aside. Whisk together eggs, cream, evaporated milk, parsley and salt; pour over top. Sprinkle with paprika. Cover and cook on low setting for 3 to 4 hours. Makes 4 to 6 servings.

Be sure to use only wood or plastic spoons in a slow cooker, to avoid scratching the crock.

Fettuccine Garden-Style

Lisa Hays
Crocker, MO

This can be served as a delicious, nutritious meatless meal.

1 zucchini, sliced 1/4-inch thick
1 yellow squash, sliced
   1/4-inch thick
2 carrots, peeled and thinly
   sliced
1-1/2 c. sliced mushrooms
10-oz. pkg. frozen broccoli cuts
4 green onions, sliced
1 clove garlic, minced

1/2 t. dried basil
1/4 t. salt
1/2 t. pepper
1 c. grated Parmesan cheese
12-oz. pkg. fettuccine pasta,
   cooked
1 c. shredded mozzarella cheese
1 c. milk
2 egg yolks, beaten

Place vegetables, seasonings and Parmesan in a slow cooker. Cover and cook on high setting for 2 hours. Add remaining ingredients to slow cooker; stir to blend well. Reduce heat to low setting; cover and cook an additional 15 to 30 minutes. Makes 6 to 8 servings.

Fluffy mashed potatoes for a crowd will stay warm and tasty for hours...just spoon them into a slow cooker set on warm.

Slow-Simmered Green Beans

Cathy Lipchak
Mechanicsville, VA

Stir in some chopped bacon for a smokey taste.

1-1/2 lbs. green beans, sliced
1 stalk celery, diced
1/4 c. onion, chopped
1/4 c. margarine, sliced

4 cubes beef bouillon
1 T. sugar
1 t. garlic salt
1/4 t. dill seed

Place all ingredients in a slow cooker; stir to mix. Cover and cook on low setting for 3 to 4 hours. Serves 6 to 8.

Grandma's Corn

Dixie Dickson
Sachse, TX

An old-timey potluck favorite.

8-oz. pkg. cream cheese
1/4 c. butter
32-oz. pkg. frozen corn

1/3 c. sugar or sugar blend
  for baking
Optional: 1 to 3 T. water

Let cream cheese and butter soften in slow cooker on low setting for about 10 minutes. Add corn and sugar or sugar substitute; stir well until corn is coated with cream cheese mixture. Cover and cook on low setting for 3 to 4 hours, stirring occasionally. If corn seems too thick, add water as needed just before serving. Serves 6 to 8.

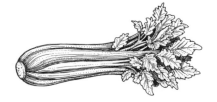

Slow and steady wins the race.

-Aesop's Fables

◆ Scrumptious Sides ◆
Tasty side dishes

Barbecued Green Beans

Kendra Walker
Hamilton, OH

A yummy picnic dish!

2 14-oz. cans green beans, drained
2 14-oz. cans French-cut green beans, drained
6 slices bacon, diced
1 onion, chopped
1 c. brown sugar, packed
1 c. catsup

Place green beans in a slow cooker; set aside. Sauté bacon in a skillet over medium heat for 3 minutes; add onion and continue cooking until bacon is crisp. Add brown sugar and catsup; stir until sugar is dissolved. Pour over beans and mix well. Cover and cook on low setting for 6 to 8 hours. Makes 4 servings.

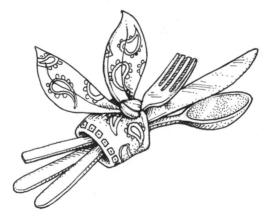

Keep a big stack of bandannas on hand to use as napkins when serving messy sandwiches!

Rose's Spaghetti Gravy

Diane Tracy
Lake Mary, FL

You won't miss the meat in this delicious pasta sauce!

2 28-oz. cans whole tomatoes,
   coarsely chopped
12-oz. can tomato paste
1/2 green pepper, chopped
1/2 red onion, chopped
1-1/2 t. dried oregano

1 t. dried basil
2 bay leaves
2 cloves garlic, minced
1 T. brown sugar, packed
salt and pepper to taste

Combine all ingredients in a slow cooker. Cover and cook on low setting for 5 to 6 hours. Adjust seasonings to taste, adding more garlic and basil if too sweet or a little more brown sugar if not sweet enough. Discard bay leaves before serving. Makes 9 to 10 cups, enough for about 2 pounds cooked spaghetti.

Coney Sauce

Cathy Young
Evansville, IN

Makes enough to satisfy a hungry team of Little Leaguers!

3 lbs. lean ground beef, browned
   and drained
28-oz. can tomato purée
1 c. onion, chopped
2 T. chili powder

1-1/2 T. mustard
1-1/2 T. Worcestershire sauce
1 T. salt
1 T. pepper
1 t. garlic powder

Combine all ingredients in a slow cooker. Cover and cook on high setting for 3 hours, stirring occasionally. Turn setting to low to keep warm. Makes enough sauce for about 20 hot dogs.

◆ Scrumptious Sides ◆
Tasty side dishes

Famous Hot Dog Chili Sauce

Debi Gilpin
Uniontown, PA

Famous among my friends...because everybody loves it!

4 c. water
1 c. catsup
6-oz. can tomato paste
1-1/2 oz. pkg. onion soup mix
3 T. brown sugar, packed
3 T. beef bouillon granules
1 T. chili powder

1-1/2 t. ground cumin
1 t. paprika
1 t. dried oregano
1/2 t. garlic salt
1/2 t. pepper
hot pepper sauce to taste

Combine all ingredients in a slow cooker. Cover and cook on high setting for 2 hours. Reduce heat to low setting, cover and cook for an additional 4 hours. Makes enough sauce for about 24 hot dogs.

Pick up a stack of vintage plastic burger baskets. Lined with red-checked paper napkins, they're still such fun for serving hot dogs, burgers and fries. Don't forget the pickle!

German Potato Salad

Maureen Laskovich
Allison Park, PA

I was looking for something new for Easter dinner when I ran across this recipe. I tried it and my family loved it!

4 c. potatoes, peeled and cubed
6 slices bacon, crisply cooked, crumbled and 2 T. drippings reserved
3/4 c. onion, chopped
10-3/4 oz. can cream of chicken soup
1/4 c. water
2 T. cider vinegar
1/2 t. sugar
pepper and dried parsley to taste

Cover potatoes with water in a saucepan; simmer over medium heat about 15 minutes, just until tender. Drain and let cool. Sauté onion in reserved drippings until tender, about 5 minutes. Blend together soup, water, vinegar, sugar and pepper in a large bowl; add bacon and onion. Add potatoes and parsley; mix well and pour into a slow cooker. Cover and cook on low setting for 4 hours. Serve warm or at room temperature. Makes 4 servings.

Old-fashioned games are great ice-breakers at parties...why not round up everyone at your next reunion for badminton or croquet?

◈ Scrumptious Sides ◈
Tasty side dishes

Calico Beans

Molly Wilson
Rapid City, SD

A favorite at carry-ins and backyard barbecues.

1/2 lb. bacon, crisply cooked
   and crumbled
32-oz. can pork & beans
16-oz. can corn, drained
16-oz. can lima beans, drained
   and rinsed

16-oz. can kidney beans,
   drained and rinsed
2 onions, chopped
3/4 c. brown sugar, packed
1 c. catsup
1 t. mustard

Combine bacon, pork & beans, corn and beans in a slow cooker; set aside. Stir together remaining ingredients; add to slow cooker and mix well. Cover and cook on low setting for 4 to 6 hours. Serves 10 to 12.

BBQ Cowboy Beans

Carrie Miller
Dry Fork, VA

Makes a great meal paired with hot buttery cornbread.

1/2 lb. ground beef, browned
   and drained
6 to 8 slices bacon, crisply
   cooked and crumbled
15-oz. can lima beans
15-oz. can kidney beans

16-oz. can pork & beans
1/2 c. barbecue sauce
1/2 c. sugar
1/2 c. brown sugar, packed
1 t. smoke-flavored cooking
   sauce

Combine all ingredients in a slow cooker; stir thoroughly. Cover and cook on low setting for 3 to 4 hours. Makes 8 servings.

Lazy Pierogie Casserole

Kelly Alderson
Erie, PA

Serve with grilled sausages…yum!

8-oz. pkg. bowtie pasta, cooked
4 to 6 potatoes, peeled and
   sliced 1/2-inch thick
2 8-oz. pkgs. shredded
   Cheddar cheese

3/4 c. butter, sliced
3/4 c. bacon, crisply cooked
   and crumbled
1 c. onion, finely chopped
salt and pepper to taste

Layer bowties and remaining ingredients in a slow cooker. Cover and cook on low setting for 7 to 8 hours. Stir gently before serving. Makes 4 to 6 servings.

Smashed Redskin Potatoes

Kay Marone
Des Moines, IA

Garnish with a sprinkle of snipped chives.

5 lbs. redskin potatoes,
   quartered
1 T. garlic, minced
3 cubes chicken bouillon
8-oz. container sour cream

8-oz. pkg. cream cheese,
   softened
1/2 c. butter, softened
salt and pepper to taste

Place potatoes, garlic and bouillon in a large saucepan; cover with water. Bring to a boil; cook just until potatoes are tender, about 15 minutes. Drain, reserving cooking liquid. Place potatoes, sour cream and cream cheese in a large bowl and mash, adding cooking liquid as needed until desired consistency is reached. Spoon into a slow cooker; cover and cook on low setting for 2 to 3 hours. Stir in butter, salt and pepper just before serving. Serves 10 to 12.

Bean Pot Medley

Melanie Hennen
Springfield, OH

This makes a lot, but it's so good that a large group will eat it up quickly! If you don't have a large bowl, just stir very gently so the beans stay whole.

15-oz. can black beans	15-oz. can black-eyed peas
15-oz. can kidney beans	1 c. green pepper, chopped
15-oz. can Great Northern beans	1 c. red pepper, chopped
15-oz. can garbanzo beans	1 c. onion, chopped

Drain and rinse all the beans and peas in a colander. Pour into a large plastic bowl with a lid; add peppers and onion. Cover bowl and shake until blended. Pour half of sauce over beans, cover and shake; add remaining sauce and shake again. Pour into a slow cooker; cover and cook on low setting for 5 to 6 hours. Makes 8 to 10 servings.

Sauce:

1-1/2 c. catsup	1/8 t. pepper
1/2 c. brown sugar, packed	2 to 3 t. red wine vinegar or
2 T. dried basil	champagne vinegar
1 t. dry mustard	

Mix all ingredients together in a medium bowl.

Sprinkle the buffet table with multi-colored confetti or sparkly sequins...set dishes in place and you're ready for a party!

Copper Kettle Apple Butter
Barbara Shultis
South Egremont, MA

Enjoy with fresh-baked bread...is there anything better?

12 c. Granny Smith apples,
   cored, peeled and quartered
1-1/2 c. brown sugar, packed
1/2 c. apple juice

1 t. allspice
1 t. nutmeg
1/2 t. ground cloves

Mix together all ingredients in a slow cooker. Cover and cook on low setting for 8 to 10 hours, or until apples are very tender. Mash apples with a fork or potato masher. Cook, uncovered, on low setting for an additional one to 2 hours, stirring occasionally until very thick. Let cool for about 2 hours; spoon into containers. Keep refrigerated for up to 3 weeks. Makes about 4 cups.

Cinnamon Spiced Applesauce
Nola Coons
Gooseberry Patch

*I've made this recipe quite often and it's always very tasty...
even kids love it! Try it over ice cream or pound
cake too...even pork chops!*

12 c. McIntosh apples, cored,
   peeled and sliced
1/2 c. sugar

1 c. water
1 T. lemon juice
1/2 t. cinnamon

Combine all ingredients in a slow cooker. Cover and cook for 5 to 7 hours on low setting, or 2-1/2 to 3-1/2 hours on high setting. Makes about 6 cups.

Spoon homemade applesauce or apple butter into a Mason jar topped with a circle of homespun. Tie a raffia bow around the top...friends will love it!

◆ Scrumptious Sides ◆
Tasty side dishes

Grandma's Fruit Compote

Debrah Veronese
Sunriver, OR

This very old-fashioned recipe was my Grandma Eva's. Many years ago, she traveled on a wagon train from Saskatchewan to Indiana, where she met Grandpa. She lived to the grand old age of 104 years!

4 apples, cored, peeled
    and cubed
4 pears, cored, peeled
    and cubed
1 c. raisins
1 c. cranberries
1 c. sugar
1/2 c. water

2 t. cinnamon
1 t. nutmeg
1 t. cardamom
13-1/2 oz. can sliced peaches
13-1/2 oz. can apricot halves
13-1/2 oz. can cherries, drained
1 c. blackberries

Combine apples, pears, raisins, cranberries, sugar, water and spices in a slow cooker. Cover and cook on low setting for 4 to 6 hours. Add canned fruit and blackberries; cover and cook on low for an additional hour. Makes 6 servings.

Set up a framed menu at your next gathering...let everyone know that delicious dishes like "Great-Grandmother's Pot Roast" and "Aunt Betty's Pudding Cake" await!

Berry Good Wild Rice

Judith Jennings
Ironwood, MI

Try it...you'll never go back to plain old white rice!

1-1/2 c. long-cooking wild rice,
   uncooked
2 14-oz. cans vegetable broth
4-1/2 oz. can sliced mushrooms
4 green onions, sliced
1 T. butter, melted

1/2 t. salt
1/4 t. pepper
1/2 c. slivered almonds
1/3 c. sweetened, dried
   cranberries

Mix all ingredients except almonds and cranberries in a slow cooker. Cover and cook on low setting for 4 to 5 hours, until rice is tender. About 30 minutes before serving time, place almonds in an ungreased heavy skillet over medium-low heat. Cook for 5 to 7 minutes, stirring frequently, until almonds begin to brown; stir constantly until golden and fragrant. Stir almonds and cranberries into rice mixture. Cover and cook on low setting an additional 15 minutes. Makes 6 servings.

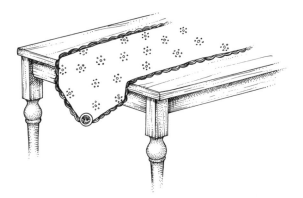

Create a table runner...a quick way to make any dinner more festive! Purchase cotton fabric in a cheerful holiday or vintage print, hem or pink the edges and you're done!

Holiday Sage Stuffing

Sonja Enright
Toms River, NJ

This recipe is great for Thanksgiving...the slow cooker
gives me an extra cooking surface.

1 c. butter
2 onions, chopped
4 stalks celery, chopped
1/4 c. fresh parsley, chopped
12 to 13 c. day-old bread, cubed
1-1/2 t. salt
1/2 t. pepper
1-1/2 t. dried sage
1 t. poultry seasoning
1 t. dried thyme
3 c. vegetable or chicken broth
2 eggs, beaten

Melt butter in a skillet over medium heat. Sauté onions, celery and parsley; pour over bread cubes in a large mixing bowl. Add seasonings and toss together. Pour broth over bread and toss again; add eggs and mix. Pack lightly in a slow cooker. Cover and cook on high setting for 45 minutes. Reduce setting to low and cook for 4 to 6 hours. Check after 2 hours; add more broth if a moister stuffing is preferred. Makes 8 to 10 servings.

Heap yellow, orange and deep green squash in a basket
for a bountiful fall centerpiece.

Country Cornbread Dressing
Tracy Chitwood
Van Buren, MO

The best dressing I've ever tasted...and so easy too!

8-oz. pan baked cornbread,
    crumbled
8 slices day-old bread, torn
4 eggs, beaten
1 onion, chopped
1/4 c. celery, chopped
2 14-1/2 oz. cans chicken broth

2 10-3/4 oz. cans cream of
    chicken soup
1-1/2 T. dried sage
1 t. salt
1/4 t. pepper
2 T. margarine, sliced

Combine all ingredients except margarine in a very large bowl; mix
well. Spoon into a slow cooker and dot with margarine. Cover and
cook on low setting for 6 to 8 hours, or on high setting for 3 to
4 hours. Makes 16 servings.

Autumn Apple-Pecan Dressing
Fawn McKenzie
Wenatchee, WA

Extra special for the holidays.

4 c. soft bread cubes
1 c. saltine crackers, crushed
1-1/2 c. apples, cored, peeled
    and chopped
1 c. chopped pecans
1 c. onion, chopped

1 c. celery, chopped
2/3 c. chicken broth
1/4 c. butter, melted
2 eggs, beaten
1/2 t. pepper
1/2 t. dried sage

Combine bread cubes, cracker crumbs, apples, pecans, onion and
celery in a slow cooker; set aside. In a small bowl, mix remaining
ingredients until well blended. Pour into slow cooker and toss to coat.
Cover and cook on low for 4 to 5 hours, until dressing is puffed and
golden around the edges. Serves 8.

Yummy Dips, Spreads & Snacks

Food to share with friends

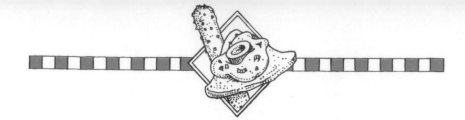

Finger-Lickin' Ribs

Brad Daugherty
Columbus, OH

Slice into individual ribs to serve as appetizers...yum!

3 to 4 lbs. baby back pork ribs
salt and pepper to taste
garlic salt to taste

8-oz. bottle Russian salad
   dressing
3/4 c. pineapple juice

Slice ribs into several portions to fit into slow cooker; sprinkle with salt and pepper. Arrange in a slow cooker; add enough water just to cover. Cover and cook on high setting for 6 to 7 hours, until tender; drain. Arrange ribs on a broiler pan and sprinkle with garlic salt. Combine salad dressing and pineapple juice in a small mixing bowl; brush ribs with half the sauce. Broil until browned; turn over, brush with remaining sauce and broil other side. Serves 8 to 10.

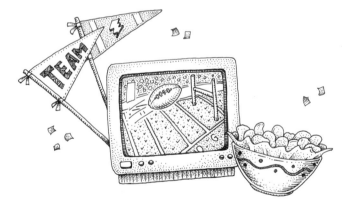

Invite friends over for snacks on game day. With hearty appetizers simmering in a slow cooker or 2, you'll be able to relax and enjoy the big game with your guests!

Yummy Dips, Spreads & Snacks
◆ Food to share with friends ◆

Spicy Honey-Molasses Wings

Connie Hilty
Pearland, TX

Irresistible at parties!

5 lbs. chicken wings
2-1/2 c. spicy catsup
2/3 c. vinegar
1/2 c. plus 2 T. honey
1/2 c. molasses
1 t. salt

1 t. Worcestershire sauce
1/2 t. onion powder
1/2 t. chili powder
Optional: 1/2 to 1 t. smoke-
   flavored cooking sauce

Arrange chicken wings in a greased 15"x10" jelly-roll pan. Bake, uncovered, at 375 degrees for 30 minutes. Drain; turn wings and bake for an additional 20 to 25 minutes. Remove wings from oven; set aside. Combine remaining ingredients in a large saucepan. Bring to a boil; reduce heat and simmer, uncovered, for 25 to 30 minutes. Arrange one-third of wings in a 5-quart slow cooker; top with one cup sauce. Repeat layers twice. Cover and cook on low setting for 3 to 4 hours; stir before serving. Makes about 4 dozen.

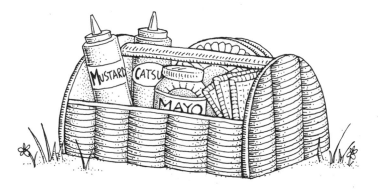

Headed outside for a backyard party? Grab a wicker garden caddy...fill it up with napkins, condiments and everything you need!

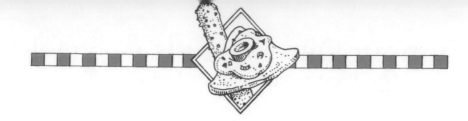

Aunt Becky's Smokey Sausages
Sandra Smith
Arleta, CA

This was one of my late sister's special recipes.

14-oz. pkg. mini smoked
    sausages
28-oz. bottle barbecue sauce
1-1/4 c. water

3 T. Worcestershire sauce
2 T. steak sauce
1/2 t. pepper

Combine all ingredients in a slow cooker; mix well. Cover and cook on low setting for 6 to 8 hours. Makes 8 servings.

Glazed Kielbasa Bites
Janice Dorsey
San Antonio, TX

So easy to double for a crowd.

1 lb. Kielbasa, sliced
1 c. apricot preserves

1/2 c. maple syrup
2 T. bourbon or apple juice

Combine all ingredients in a slow cooker. Cover and cook on low setting for 4 hours. Serves 8 to 10.

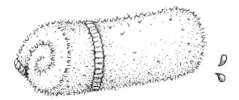

Serving yummy-but-sticky finger foods? Fill a mini slow cooker set on low with rolled-up, dampened fingertip towels...guests will appreciate your thoughtfulness!

Yummy Dips, Spreads & Snacks
Food to share with friends

Tipsy Dogs

Shirley McGlin
Black Creek, WI

I always make these at the holidays...so easy to stir up!

2 1-lb. pkgs. mini cocktail
   wieners
2 c. catsup
3/4 c. brown sugar, packed
1 T. mustard

1/4 c. vinegar
1 onion, chopped
1/2 c. beer
Optional: hot pepper sauce

Combine all ingredients in a slow cooker. Cover and cook on low setting for 30 minutes to one hour, until hot. Serves 18 to 20.

Saucy Kielbasa

Catherine Abbott
East Providence, RI

An old friend shared this simple recipe with me.

2 lbs. Kielbasa
2 8-oz. jars Dijon mustard

3 10-oz. jars currant jelly

Cover Kielbasa with water in a medium saucepan; bring to a boil over medium-high heat. Simmer for 15 to 20 minutes; drain and cut into bite-size pieces. Combine all ingredients in a slow cooker. Cover and cook on low setting for one to 2 hours, until heated through. Serves 18 to 20.

Serve icy cold
beverages in pint-size
Mason jars
just for fun!

Bacon-Horseradish Dip

Kathy Grashoff
Fort Wayne, IN

It's out of this world!

3 8-oz. pkgs. cream cheese,
   cubed and softened
12-oz. pkg. shredded Cheddar
   cheese
1 c. half-and-half
1/3 c. green onion, chopped
3 cloves garlic, minced

3 T. prepared horseradish
1 T. Worcestershire sauce
1/2 t. pepper
12 slices bacon, crisply cooked
   and crumbled
bagel chips or assorted crackers

Combine all ingredients except bacon and chips or crackers in a slow cooker. Cover and cook on low setting for 4 to 5 hours, or on high setting for 2 to 2-1/2 hours, stirring once halfway through. Stir in bacon; serve with corn chips or crackers. Makes 7 to 8 cups.

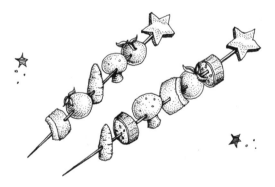

Thread bite-size veggies like cherry tomatoes, whole mushrooms, yellow pepper squares and baby carrots onto skewers for tasty dipping. Stand skewers in a plump vase...it doubles as a table decoration!

Yummy Dips, Spreads & Snacks
◆ Food to share with friends ◆

Mom's Slow-Cooker Mini Reubens

Cheryl Breeden
North Platte, NE

*This was always my mom's favorite recipe during football season...
even if our team lost, dinner was always a winner!*

1/4 to 1/2 lb. deli corned beef,
   chopped
2 16-oz. pkgs. shredded Swiss
   cheese
8-oz. bottle Thousand Island
   salad dressing

32-oz. pkg. refrigerated
   sauerkraut, drained and
   chopped
Optional: 1 t. caraway seed
1 to 2 loaves party rye bread
Garnish: dill pickle slices

Put all ingredients except party rye and pickles in a slow cooker. Cover and cook on low setting for about 4 hours, or until mixture is hot and cheese is melted. Stir to blend well. To serve, arrange party rye slices and pickles on separate plates around slow cooker. Makes 10 to 12 servings.

Having a potluck party? Ask everyone ahead of time to share the recipe they'll be bringing. Make copies of all the recipes and staple into a booklet...a thoughtful party souvenir!

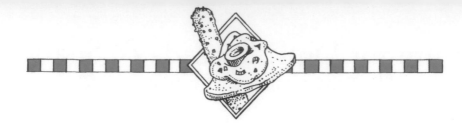

Tropical Tea

Angela Murphy
Tempe, AZ

A delightful, warming beverage for a cool day.

6 c. boiling water
6 teabags
1-1/2 c. unsweetened pineapple
   juice

1-1/2 c. orange juice
1/3 c. sugar
2 T. honey
1 orange, halved and sliced

Combine boiling water and teabags in a slow cooker; cover and let steep for 5 minutes. Discard teabags; stir in remaining ingredients. Cover and cook on low setting for 2 to 4 hours, until heated through. Serve in mugs or teacups. Makes about 2-1/2 quarts.

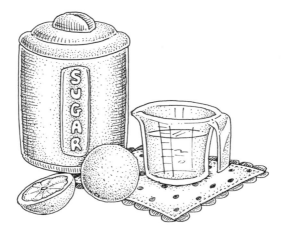

Look for small muslin drawstring bags at shops where loose tea is sold...they're just right for enclosing whole spices in slow-cooker beverages.

Yummy Dips, Spreads & Snacks
◆ Food to share with friends ◆

Spiced Chocolate Coffee

Regina Vining
Warwick, RI

Top with sweetened whipped cream for a special treat.

8 c. brewed coffee
1/3 c. sugar
1/4 c. chocolate syrup

4 4-inch cinnamon sticks
1-1/2 t. whole cloves

Combine first 3 ingredients in a slow cooker; set aside. Wrap spices in a coffee filter and tie with kitchen string; add to slow cooker. Cover and cook on low setting for 2 to 3 hours. Remove and discard spices. Ladle coffee into mugs. Makes 6 to 8 servings.

Watch yard sales for a vintage salad dressing server...it's just as handy for offering up a variety of coffee stir-ins to guests!

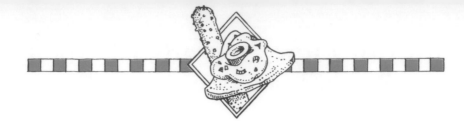

Family Favorite Party Mix ▶ *Courtney Robinson*
Worthington, OH

Fill up small plastic bags with this tasty mix and tie with curling ribbon for a merry take-home treat.

1 c. bite-size crispy wheat
   cereal squares
1 c. bite-size crispy rice
   cereal squares
1 c. bite-size crispy corn
   cereal squares
1 c. peanuts

1 c. pretzel sticks
1/4 c. butter, melted
2 T. Worcestershire sauce
1 t. seasoned salt
1 t. garlic salt
1 c. candy-coated chocolates
1 c. raisins

Combine cereals, peanuts and pretzels in a slow cooker; set aside. Mix together butter, Worcestershire sauce and salts; gently stir into cereal mixture. Cover and cook on low setting for 3 to 4 hours. Uncover and cook on low setting for an additional 30 minutes, stirring occasionally. Drain mix on paper towel-lined baking sheets; transfer to a large bowl. Cool. Add candy-coated chocolates and raisins; toss to mix. Store in an airtight container. Makes 7 cups.

Paper muffin cup liners come in all colors and even holiday designs...great for serving individual portions of party mix!

Yummy Dips, Spreads & Snacks
◆ Food to share with friends ◆

Cinnamon-Cocoa Granola

Melody Taynor
Everett, WA

A tasty nibble that's healthy too!

4 c. long-cooking oats,
   uncooked
2/3 c. honey
1 c. bran cereal
1 c. wheat germ

1/2 c. sesame seed
1/4 c. oil
2 T. baking cocoa
1 t. cinnamon

Combine all ingredients in a slow cooker. Cook on low setting with lid slightly ajar for about 4 hours, stirring occasionally. Cool; store in an airtight container for one to 2 weeks. Makes about 6 cups.

Turn an old vinyl record album into a whimsical snack bowl! Center it on an inverted heat-proof mixing bowl and set on a baking sheet. Bake at 300 degrees for about 5 minutes, until the record softens. Using oven mitts, carefully and gently shape the plastic. Set on a hotpad to cool.

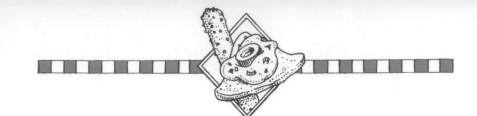

Hot Buffalo Dip
Vickie

One of my favorite party dips...oh-so easy to make and we all love it!

3 to 4 boneless, skinless chicken
    breasts, cooked and chopped
1 c. hot wing sauce
2 8-oz. pkgs. cream cheese,
    cubed and softened

1/2 c. shredded Cheddar cheese
1/4 c. blue cheese salad dressing
corn chips, celery stalks

In a slow cooker, mix together all ingredients except corn chips and celery stalks. Cover and cook on low setting for 3 to 4 hours. Serve with corn chips and celery stalks for dipping. Makes 8 to 10 servings.

Curl the ends of chenille stems around a pencil and
tuck into a bouquet of fresh-cut zinnias or daisies for
a whimsical accent.

Yummy Dips, Spreads & Snacks
◆◆ Food to share with friends ◆◆

South-of-the-Border Dip

Tonya Lewis
Crothersville, IN

It's like a fiesta in your slow cooker!

1 lb. ground beef
1 lb. ground pork sausage
10-3/4 oz. can cream of
   mushroom soup
16-oz. pkg. Mexican pasteurized
   process cheese spread, cubed
4-oz. can chopped green chiles
tortilla chips

Brown ground beef and sausage in a skillet; drain. Combine with soup, cheese and chiles in a slow cooker. Cover and cook on low setting for 3 to 4 hours, until cheese is melted. Serve with tortilla chips. Makes 7 to 8 cups.

Rosemarie's Chili-Cheese Dip

Shirley Padilla
Houston, TX

My mom started making this years ago. We love it on hot dogs,
baked potatoes and broccoli as well as corn chips...my favorite way!

1-1/2 lbs. ground beef,
   browned and drained
2 10-oz. cans tomatoes
   with chiles
1-1/4 oz. pkg. chili
   seasoning mix
32-oz pkg. pasteurized process
   cheese spread, cubed

Mix together ground beef, tomatoes and seasoning in a slow cooker and set aside. Place cheese in a microwave-safe bowl. Microwave on high setting for 5 to 6 minutes until melted, stirring after 3 minutes. Add cheese to ground beef mixture. Cover and cook briefly on low setting until warmed through, stirring occasionally. Keep warm in slow cooker. Makes 9 to 10 cups.

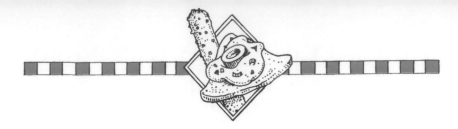

Chili Chicken Wings

Jason Keller
Carrollton, GA

A tailgating tradition.

4 lbs. chicken wings
12-oz. bottle chili sauce

3 to 4 T. hot pepper sauce

Arrange wings on a broiler pan. Broil 4 to 5 inches from heat until golden, about 10 minutes, turning to cook evenly. Transfer wings to a slow cooker. Combine sauces and pour over wings. Cover and cook on low setting for 4 to 5 hours, or on high setting for 2 to 2-1/2 hours. Serve with Blue Cheese Dip. Makes 3 to 4 dozen.

Blue Cheese Dip:

3/4 c. mayonnaise
1/2 c. sour cream
1/2 c. crumbled blue cheese
2 T. fresh parsley, minced

1 T. lemon juice
1 T. white vinegar
1 clove garlic, minced
salt and pepper

Combine all ingredients; chill for one to 2 hours.

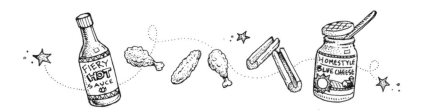

Make it easy for guests to mingle and chat...set up food at several tables instead of one big party buffet. Place hot foods on one table, chilled foods at another, sweets at yet another.

Yummy Dips, Spreads & Snacks

◆ Food to share with friends ◆

Honey Chicken Wings

Karen Mooney
Newnan, GA

You won't "bee"-lieve how scrumptious these are!

3 lbs. chicken wings
salt and pepper
2 c. honey
1 c. soy sauce

1/2 c. catsup
1/4 c. oil
2 cloves garlic, minced

Sprinkle wings with salt and pepper. Arrange on a broiler pan;
broil 4 to 5 inches from heat until golden, about 10 minutes per side.
Transfer wings to a slow cooker and set aside. Combine remaining
ingredients in a small bowl; pour over wings. Cover and cook on low
setting for 4 to 5 hours, or on high setting for 2 to 2-1/2 hours.
Makes about 2-1/2 dozen.

Place whole cinnamon sticks, cloves and strips of orange
peel in a mini slow cooker. Add 2 to 3 cups water and
simmer on low setting. Your whole house will smell sweet!

Fruited Rum Punch

Nancy Wise
Little Rock, AR

This punch will put you right in the holiday spirit!

2 qts. apple cider
2 c. pineapple juice
1 c. orange juice
1 c. lemon juice
1 c. cranberry juice cocktail

3 4-inch cinnamon sticks
1 T. whole cloves
1/4 c. sugar
Optional: rum

Combine all ingredients except rum in a slow cooker. Cover and cook on low setting for 6 to 8 hours. Ladle punch into mugs and add a shot of rum to each mug, if desired. Makes 14 servings.

Hot Grape Punch

Katherine Nelson
Centerville, UT

A great addition to any winter get-together.

12 whole cloves
4 c. grape juice
2 T. lemon juice

2 4-inch cinnamon sticks
2 c. water

Place cloves in a tea strainer or tie in cheese cloth. Combine all ingredients in a slow cooker; cover and cook on low for 5 to 6 hours. Discard spices before serving. Serves 6.

Don't take life too
seriously...laugh and smile
at it once in awhile.
-Unknown

Yummy Dips, Spreads & Snacks
◆◆ Food to share with friends ◆◆

Mocha Cocoa

Vickie

Just about the best cocoa you've ever tasted!

8-oz. pkg. semi-sweet baking
   chocolate, chopped
3 c. half-and-half
2 c. milk
1 c. strong brewed coffee
2 T. brown sugar, packed
1 t. vanilla extract

1 t. cinnamon
1/2 t. allspice
1/2 t. nutmeg
1/8 t. salt
Garnish: 1 c. whipping cream,
   whipped

Combine all ingredients except whipping cream in a slow cooker; mix well. Cover and cook on high setting for one hour, until chocolate is melted, stirring every 15 minutes. Serve immediately, or reduce to low setting and keep covered. Top individual mugs with a dollop of whipped cream. Serves 6.

Snowy Day Hot Chocolate

Dana Iungerich
Frisco, TX

Serve with peppermint sticks for stirring.

14-oz. can sweetened
   condensed milk
1/2 c. baking cocoa

2 t. vanilla extract
6-1/2 c. hot water
Garnish: marshmallows

Combine condensed milk, cocoa and vanilla in a slow cooker, mixing well with a whisk. Gradually stir in hot water, mixing well. Cover and cook on low setting for 3 to 4 hours, stirring occasionally. Top individual servings with marshmallows. Makes about 8 servings.

Fill up a slow cooker with hot chocolate before going out to enjoy snowy winter weather...what could be cozier when you return home?

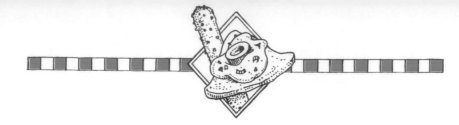

Swedish Meatballs

Jody Thiel
Ripon, WI

Makes a delicious dinner too...just serve over buttery noodles.

1 lb. ground beef
1 onion, chopped
6 graham crackers, finely
    crushed
1 T. sugar

1 t. salt
1/2 t. pepper
3 to 4 t. milk
10-1/2 oz. can beef broth

Combine all ingredients except broth in a large bowl. Mix well, adding a little extra milk if mixture appears too dry. Form into one-inch balls. Cook meatballs in a lightly greased skillet over medium heat until lightly browned, turning frequently. Remove meatballs from skillet; arrange in a slow cooker and set aside. Add broth to drippings in skillet; cook and stir over medium heat until slightly thickened. Pour broth mixture over meatballs; cover and cook on high setting for one hour. Serves 6.

Make some amusing party picks in no time! Attach tiny, shiny ornament balls to long toothpicks with craft glue, just for fun!

Yummy Dips, Spreads & Snacks
◆ Food to share with friends ◆

Kathy's Dilly Meatballs

Jennifer Heinl
Pittsburgh, PA

*This recipe is from my mom, who taught me that
a slow cooker is a busy girl's best friend!*

3 lbs. ground beef
1-1/2 c. dry bread crumbs
3/4 c. milk
3 eggs
1 onion, finely chopped
1 T. salt
1/4 t. pepper

1-1/2 t. Worcestershire sauce
3 10-3/4 oz. cans cream of
    chicken soup
1 c. milk
1 t. dill weed
1-1/2 c. sour cream
Garnish: fresh parsley, snipped

Combine first 8 ingredients in a large bowl. Form into one-inch balls;
arrange on an ungreased 15"x10" jelly-roll pan. Bake at 350 degrees
for 25 to 30 minutes, until lightly browned; drain and set aside.
Combine soup, milk and dill in a slow cooker; add meatballs. Cover
and cook on high setting until boiling, about 30 minutes, stirring
occasionally. Reduce to low setting; cover and cook for one hour. Stir
in sour cream; heat through. Sprinkle with parsley. Serves 15 to 20.

A party buffet looks oh-so
inviting when risers
are used to raise up
serving bowls and baskets.
Arrange upside-down
cake pans or shallow
dishes and drape with a
tablecloth, then set food
containers on top.

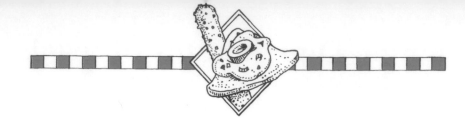

Sugared Walnuts

Connie Fortune
Covington, OH

Pecans are yummy too!

16-oz. pkg. walnut halves
1/2 c. butter, melted
1/2 c. powdered sugar

1-1/2 t. cinnamon
1/4 t. ground cloves
1/4 t. ground ginger

Preheat slow cooker on high setting for about 15 minutes. Add nuts and butter, stirring to mix well. Add powdered sugar; mix until coated evenly. Cover and cook on high setting for 15 minutes. Reduce heat to low setting. Cook, uncovered, stirring occasionally, for 2 to 3 hours, or until nuts are coated with a crisp glaze. Transfer nuts to a serving bowl; set aside. Combine spices in a small bowl and sprinkle over nuts, stirring to coat evenly. Cool before serving. Store in an airtight container. Serves 12 to 16.

Fill a Chinese takeout container with yummy
Sugared Walnuts or Cajun Spiced Pecans...always
a welcome hostess gift!

Yummy Dips, Spreads & Snacks
Food to share with friends ◆

Cajun Spiced Pecans

Kerry Mayer
Dunham Springs, LA

Fill small ribbon-tied bags with these delightful nuts to send home with guests as party favors.

16-oz. pkg. pecan halves
1/4 c. butter, melted
1 T. chili powder
1 t. dried basil
1 t. dried oregano

1 t. dried thyme
1 t. salt
1/2 t. onion powder
1/4 t. garlic powder
1/4 t. cayenne pepper

Combine all ingredients in a slow cooker. Cover and cook on high setting for 15 minutes. Turn to low setting and cook, uncovered, for 2 hours, stirring occasionally. Transfer nuts to a baking sheet; cool completely. Store in an airtight container. Serves 12 to 16.

Sweet or spicy nuts make a tasty, crunchy salad garnish...
just coarsely chop and sprinkle on!

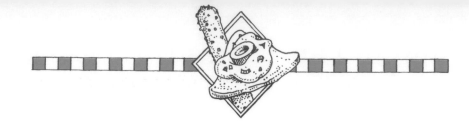

Hot Crab Dip

Betty McKay
Harmony, MN

Perfect for card clubs and open houses.

1/2 c. milk
1/3 c. salsa
3 8-oz. pkgs. cream cheese,
   cubed

2 8-oz. pkgs. imitation
   crabmeat, flaked
1 c. green onion, sliced
assorted crackers

Combine milk and salsa in a slow cooker; stir in remaining ingredients except crackers. Cover and cook for 3 to 4 hours on low setting, stirring every 30 minutes. Serve with crackers. Makes about 5 cups.

Creamy Seafood Dip

Lynda Robson
Boston, MA

Add a little more crabmeat or shrimp if you prefer not to use lobster.

2 10-3/4 cans cream of
   celery soup
2 c. sharp pasteurized process
   cheese, grated
8-oz. pkg. imitation crabmeat,
   flaked
1/2 c. cooked lobster, diced

1/2 c. cooked shrimp, chopped
1/8 t. paprika
1/8 t. nutmeg
1/8 t. cayenne pepper
1 loaf crusty bread, cut into
   1-inch cubes

Combine all ingredients except bread; stir well. Cover and cook on low setting for 2 hours, or until cheese is melted. Serve with bread cubes for dipping. Makes 6 to 7 cups.

Scatter colored marbles or flat glass beads in a punch bowl and fill with water. Add floating tealights...magical!

Yummy Dips, Spreads & Snacks
◆ Food to share with friends ◆

Crabby Artichoke Spread

Kathy Grashoff
Fort Wayne, IN

Your guests will just love this creamy, spicy dip!

1 jalapeño pepper, seeded
   and chopped
1 t. oil
14-oz. can artichokes, drained
   and chopped
6-oz. can crabmeat, drained
1/2 red pepper, chopped

2 green onions, chopped
1 c. mayonnaise
1/4 c. grated Parmesan cheese
2 t. lemon juice
2 t. Worcestershire sauce
1/2 t. celery seed
assorted crackers

In a skillet over medium heat, sauté jalapeño in oil until tender.
Combine in a slow cooker with remaining ingredients except crackers.
Cover and cook on low setting for 4 to 6 hours. Serve with crackers.
Makes 3 to 4 cups.

Creamy hot dips are twice as tasty with homemade
baguette crisps! Thinly slice a French loaf and arrange
slices on a baking sheet. Sprinkle with olive oil and garlic
powder, then bake at 400 degrees for 12 to 15 minutes.

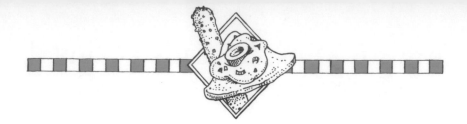

Bacon-Dog Roll-Ups

Diana Chaney
Olathe, KS

Guests will sit up and beg for these tasty tidbits!

1 lb. bacon, cut into thirds
2 1-lb. pkgs. mini cocktail
   wieners

1/2 to 3/4 c. brown sugar,
   packed

Wrap bacon slices around wieners; secure with toothpicks. Arrange one layer of wrapped wieners in bottom of slow cooker; sprinkle generously with brown sugar. Repeat layering, ending with more brown sugar. Cover and cook on low setting for 5 to 6 hours, or on high setting for 3 to 4 hours. Makes about 5 dozen.

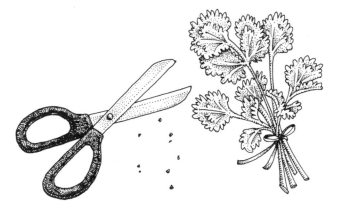

Keep a pair of kitchen shears handy. They make short work of snipping herbs, dicing bacon or even cutting cheese slices into shreds.

Ooey-Gooey Desserts

Warm & cozy delights

Chocolate-Peanut Butter Cake

Lisa Hays
Crocker, MO

Sprinkle with chocolate chips while it's still warm
for a yummy topping.

18-1/2 oz. pkg. chocolate
   cake mix
1/2 c. water

1/3 c. creamy peanut butter
1/2 c. chopped peanuts

Combine all ingredients in a bowl, mixing well; beat by hand for
2 minutes. Pour into a greased and floured 2-pound metal coffee
can. Place can in a slow cooker; cover top of can with 8 paper towels
to absorb condensation. Cover and cook on high setting for 2 to
3 hours. Serves 8 to 10.

If a baking recipe calls for an empty coffee can but you
don't have one handy, any straight-sided deep cake pan or
casserole dish that fits into your slow cooker can be used.

Hot Fudge Spoon Cake

Sara Plott
Monument, CO

Heavenly!

1 c. all-purpose flour
1-3/4 c. light brown sugar,
    packed and divided
1/4 c. plus 3 T. baking cocoa,
    divided
2 t. baking powder

1/4 t. salt
1/2 c. milk
2 T. butter, melted
1/2 t. vanilla extract
1-3/4 c. hot water
Garnish: vanilla ice cream

Combine flour, one cup brown sugar, 3 tablespoons cocoa, baking powder and salt in a medium bowl. Whisk in milk, melted butter and vanilla. Spread evenly in a slow cooker. Mix together remaining brown sugar and cocoa; sprinkle evenly over top of batter. Pour in hot water; do not stir. Cover and cook on high setting for 2 hours, until a toothpick inserted one inch deep comes out clean. Spoon warm cake into bowls; top with vanilla ice cream. Makes 6 servings.

Enjoy scrumptious desserts in the summer without heating up the kitchen...bake them in a slow cooker!

Bananas Foster

Jo Ann

Guests will flip over this decadent dessert!

1/2 c. butter, melted
1/4 c. brown sugar, packed
6 bananas, cut into 1-inch slices

1/4 c. rum or 1/4 t. rum extract
Garnish: vanilla ice cream

Stir together butter, brown sugar, bananas and rum or extract in a slow cooker. Cover and cook on low setting for one hour. To serve, spoon over scoops of ice cream. Makes 4 servings.

Caramel-Rum Fondue

Ellie Brandel
Clackamas, OR

Makes a scrumptious ending to a slow-cooker appetizer party.

25 caramels, unwrapped
1/3 c. whipping cream
1/4 c. mini marshmallows

2 t. rum or 1/4 t. rum extract
apple wedges, pound cake
  squares

Combine caramels and cream in a slow cooker. Cover and cook on low setting until melted, 30 minutes to one hour. Stir in marshmallows and rum or extract. Cover and cook an additional 30 minutes. Serve with apple wedges or cake squares for dipping. Serves 6 to 8.

The long, sweet hours that bring us
all things good.

-Alfred, Lord Tennyson

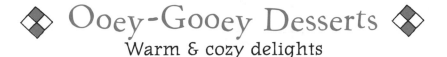

◆ Ooey-Gooey Desserts ◆
Warm & cozy delights

Cinnamon Streusel Cake

Sharon Jones
Oklahoma City, OK

A delightful brunch treat too.

16-oz. pkg. pound cake mix
1/4 c. brown sugar, packed
1 T. all-purpose flour

1 t. cinnamon
1/4 c. nuts, finely chopped
Garnish: ice cream

Prepare cake mix batter according to package directions. Pour into a generously greased and floured 2-pound metal coffee can. Mix sugar, flour, cinnamon and nuts; sprinkle over batter. Cover can with 6 to 8 paper towels to absorb condensation; place in a slow cooker. Cover and cook on high setting for 3 to 4 hours. Serve with a scoop of ice cream. Makes 10 servings.

Many slow-cooker recipes can be speeded up by cooking on high for half the time specified on low setting. For best results with slow-cooker baking, though, use the setting that the recipe calls for.

Peachy Good Dessert

Tina Schroer
Jefferson City, MO

*My husband and children just love this for breakfast as well as
dessert! If there's any left, it's yummy over ice cream.*

1/3 c. biscuit baking mix
2/3 c. quick-cooking oats,
   uncooked
1/2 c. sugar

1/2 c. brown sugar, packed
1/2 t. cinnamon
4 c. peaches, pitted, peeled
   and sliced

Mix dry ingredients together. Toss with peaches and pour into a
slow cooker that has been sprayed with non-stick vegetable spray.
Cover and cook on low setting for 4 to 6 hours. Makes 6 to 8 servings.

Dollop fresh whipped cream on warm slow-cooker
desserts...irresistible! Pour a pint of whipping cream
into a deep, narrow bowl. Beat with an electric mixer
on medium speed, gradually increasing to high speed.
When soft peaks form, add sugar to taste.

Ooey-Gooey Desserts
Warm & cozy delights

Double-Berry Cobbler

Becky Weatherman
Mocksville, NC

First I went blackberry picking with a friend...we had so much fun, even though we had to fight off wasps! Then I picked blueberries at another friend's house, only to find her dog Bruno was eating berries as fast as I could pick them...but it was worth it!

1 c. all-purpose flour
1-1/2 c. sugar, divided
1 t. baking powder
1/4 t. salt
1/4 t. cinnamon
1/4 t. nutmeg
2 eggs, beaten
2 T. milk

2 T. oil
2 c. blackberries
2 c. blueberries
3/4 c. water
1 t. orange zest
Optional: ice cream or
    whipped topping

Combine flour, 3/4 cup sugar, baking powder, salt and spices in a medium bowl; set aside. In a small bowl, combine eggs, milk and oil; stir into flour mixture until moistened. Spread batter evenly in a slow cooker; set aside. Combine berries, water, zest and remaining sugar in a large saucepan. Bring to a boil; remove from heat and pour over batter without stirring. Cover and cook on high setting for 2 to 2-1/2 hours, or until a toothpick inserted in the center tests clean. Uncover and let stand 30 minutes. Spoon into bowls, topped with ice cream or whipped topping, if desired. Makes 6 servings.

Roll up plastic cutlery in paper napkins and stack in a child's vintage sandpail...oh-so easy for party guests to grab & go!

Cozy Apple Bread Pudding

Roseann Floura
Rockwall, TX

Sprinkle with a dash of cinnamon.

8 to 9 slices cinnamon-raisin
    bread, cubed
3 eggs, beaten
2 c. milk

1/2 c. sugar
21-oz. can apple pie filling
Optional: whipped cream or
    ice cream

Spread bread cubes in a single layer on an ungreased baking sheet.
Bake at 300 degrees for 10 to 15 minutes until dry, stirring twice.
Cool. In a large bowl, whisk eggs, milk and sugar. Gently stir in pie
filling and bread cubes. Pour into a slow cooker that has been sprayed
with non-stick vegetable spray. Cover and cook on low setting for
3 hours, or until puffy and a knife inserted near the center comes out
clean. Uncover and let stand for 30 to 45 minutes; pudding will fall
as it cools. Spoon into dessert dishes; garnish as desired. Serves 6.

For quick & easy table decorations, place round pebbles
in the bottom of Mason jars and fill with water. Then
tuck in bunches of sweet daisies and tie a bow around
jar necks with jute.

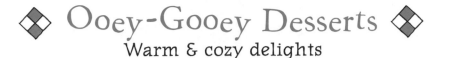

Favorite Caramel Apples

Graceann Frederico
Irondequoit, NY

Press candy-coated chocolates, candy corn, red cinnamon candies or chocolate chips into the warm caramel for a special treat.

2 14-oz. pkgs. caramels,
   unwrapped
1/4 c. water

1/2 t. cinnamon
8 apples
8 wooden skewers

Combine caramels, water and cinnamon in a slow cooker. Cover and cook on high setting for one to 1-1/2 hours, stirring frequently. Insert sticks into apples. Turn slow cooker to low. Dip apples into hot caramel and turn to coat, scraping excess caramel from bottom of apples. Place on greased wax paper to cool. Makes 8.

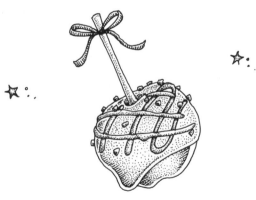

Make caramel apples extra special! Place
semi-sweet chocolate chips in a plastic zipping bag.
Microwave briefly on high setting until chocolate melts,
then snip off a small corner of bag and drizzle over apples.

Unbelievable Caramel Pie

Judy Collins
Nashville, TN

Here in Nashville, one of the country clubs always served the most delicious caramel pie. This is such an easy way to get that wonderful caramel taste!

2 14-oz. cans sweetened
   condensed milk
9-inch graham cracker crust

Garnish: whipped topping,
   mini semi-sweet
   chocolate chips

Pour condensed milk into a slow cooker that has been sprayed with non-stick vegetable spray. Cover and cook on low setting for 3-1/2 to 4 hours. After 2-1/2 hours, milk will begin to thicken; begin stirring every 15 minutes. When thick and golden, stir again until smooth; pour into crust and chill. Garnish with whipped topping and chocolate chips. Makes 6 to 8 servings.

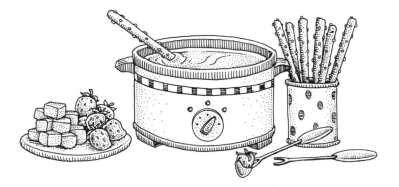

Chocolate fondue is yummy and so easy!
Simply melt chocolate chips in a mini slow cooker set
on low. Set out a platter of dippers like pretzel rods,
cubed pound cake and juicy red strawberries. Mmm!

Peanutty Clusters

Margaret Erhardt
Beavercreek, OH

Drop by spoonfuls into mini paper muffin cup liners for a special candy box finish.

2 lbs. white melting chocolate, chopped
4 1-oz. sqs. bittersweet baking chocolate squares, chopped

12-oz. pkg. semi-sweet chocolate chips
24-oz. jar dry-roasted peanuts

Combine chocolates in a slow cooker. Cover and cook on high setting for one hour. Reduce setting to low; cover and cook an additional hour, or until chocolates are melted, stirring every 15 minutes. Stir in peanuts. Drop by teaspoonfuls onto wax paper; let stand until set. Store covered at room temperature. Makes 3 to 4 dozen pieces.

Fill icing cones with homemade candies and tie with curling ribbon, then heap in a pretty basket. Guests will love choosing one as a party favor!

Fudgy Pudding Cake

Carol McMillion
Catawba, VA

This is scrumpdelicious! A friend brought it to the last 2 covered dish dinners at our church...it disappeared very quickly!

18-1/2 oz. pkg. chocolate
    cake mix
3.9-oz. pkg. instant chocolate
    pudding mix
16-oz. container sour cream
3/4 c. oil

4 eggs
1 c. water
6-oz. pkg. semi-sweet
    chocolate chips
Garnish: vanilla ice cream

Mix together all ingredients except ice cream. Pour into a slow cooker that has been sprayed with non-stick vegetable spray. Cover and cook on low setting for 6 to 8 hours. Turn off slow cooker and let stand 20 to 30 minutes; do not lift lid until ready to serve. Serve with vanilla ice cream. Makes 8 to 10 servings.

Spoon generous portions of a warm, gooey dessert into stemmed glasses and dollop with whipped topping...a sweet ending that your guests will long remember!

Raspberry Brownies in a Jar

Laurie Wilson
Fort Wayne, IN

It's fun to give these brownies in their jars as gifts...my family just loves them!

1/2 c. butter, sliced
2 1-oz. sqs. unsweetened
 baking chocolate, chopped
2 eggs, beaten
3/4 c. sugar
1/3 c. seedless raspberry jam

1 t. vanilla extract
3/4 c. all-purpose flour
1/4 t. baking powder
2 1-pt. wide-mouth canning jars
 and lids, sterilized

Grease and flour canning jars; set aside. Melt butter and chocolate together in a medium saucepan over low heat. Remove from heat; stir in eggs, sugar, jam and vanilla. Beat lightly with a spoon until combined. Stir in flour and baking powder; pour into prepared jars. Cover jars tightly with greased aluminum foil, greased-side down. Place jars in a slow cooker; pour one cup water around jars. Cover and cook on high for 3 to 3-1/2 hours, or until a toothpick inserted in center tests clean. Remove jars from slow cooker; cool for 10 minutes. Use a metal spatula to loosen brownies; turn out of jars. Cool brownies completely on a wire rack before slicing. Makes 12 servings.

Invite your best girlfriends to share the latest giggles and gossip over dessert...what a great way to get caught up on cherished friendships!

Banana Bread

Ellie Brandel
Clackamas, OR

A small loaf pan can be used if your slow cooker is oval.

1/3 c. shortening
1/2 c. sugar
2 eggs
1-3/4 c. all-purpose flour
1 t. baking powder

1/2 t. baking soda
1/2 t. salt
1 c. bananas, mashed
1/2 c. raisins

Blend together shortening and sugar in a mixing bowl; add eggs and beat well. Add dry ingredients alternately with bananas; stir in raisins. Pour batter into a greased 4-cup metal coffee can. Cover top of can with 6 to 8 paper towels to absorb condensation; set on a rack in slow cooker. Cover and cook on high setting for 2 to 3 hours, or until bread is done. Let cool slightly; turn out of can to finish cooling. Makes one loaf.

Line a vintage tin lunchbox with a pretty tea towel, add a loaf of fruit & nut bread and some spiced teabags. Hand-deliver to a friend for a gift that really says, "I've been thinking of you!"

Zucchini-Walnut Bread

Lisa Ragland
Columbus, OH

With this tasty recipe, there's no such thing as too many zucchini!

2 eggs
2/3 c. oil
1-1/4 c. sugar
2 t. vanilla extract
1-1/3 c. zucchini, peeled
   and shredded

2 c. all-purpose flour
1/2 t. baking powder
1 t. cinnamon
1/2 t. nutmeg
1/4 t. salt
1/2 to 1 c. chopped walnuts

In a mixing bowl, beat eggs until light and foamy with an electric mixer on high speed. Add oil, sugar, vanilla and zucchini; mix well and set aside. Mix remaining ingredients in another bowl; add to egg mixture and mix well. Pour into a greased and floured 2-pound metal coffee can or a 2-quart mold. Cover top with 8 paper towels to absorb condensation; set in a slow cooker. Cover and bake on high setting for 3 to 4 hours. Let stand 5 minutes before unmolding. Makes one loaf.

Create a festive centerpiece in a jiffy! Arrange mini vases around the edges of a cake plate and tuck a bright-colored blossom into each. Set a larger vase of several blossoms in the center.

Slow-Cooked Apple Pie

Mandy Bridges
Tunnel Hill, GA

Serve with a pitcher of fresh cream for drizzling...yummy!

8 Granny Smith apples, cored,
    peeled and sliced
1-1/4 t. cinnamon
1/4 t. allspice
1/4 t. nutmeg
1-1/2 c. biscuit baking mix,
    divided

3/4 c. milk
2 T. butter, softened
3/4 c. sugar
2 eggs, beaten
2 t. vanilla extract
1/3 c. brown sugar, packed
3 T. butter, chilled

Toss apple slices with spices in a large bowl; place in a lightly greased slow cooker. Combine 1/2 cup baking mix, milk, butter, sugar, eggs and vanilla; mix and spoon over apples. Combine remaining baking mix with brown sugar; cut in cold butter until crumbly. Sprinkle over apple mixture. Cover and cook on low setting for 6 to 7 hours, until apples are tender. Makes 6 servings.

Jazzed-up placecards in a hurry! Simply fold tinted index cards in half and glue on rick rack, buttons, tiny bows or scrapbooking charms...done!

Pumpkin Pie Pudding

Rhonda Reeder
Ellicott City, MD

Almost as good as Grandma's...practically bakes itself!

15-oz. can pumpkin
12-oz. can evaporated milk
3/4 c. sugar
1/2 c. biscuit baking mix
2 eggs, beaten

2 T. butter, melted
2-1/2 t. pumpkin pie spice
Optional: frozen whipped
   topping, thawed

Mix together all ingredients except whipped topping; pour into a greased slow cooker. Cover and cook on low setting for 6 to 7 hours. Serve with whipped topping, if desired. Makes 8 servings.

Pumpkin Patch Cake

Lynn Williams
Muncie, IN

An extra special ending to a holiday dinner.

1/2 c. sugar
1/2 c. dark brown sugar, packed
1/2 c. oil
2 eggs, beaten
1 c. canned pumpkin
1-1/2 c. all-purpose flour

1/2 t. salt
1/2 t. cinnamon
1 t. pumpkin pie spice
1 t. baking soda
1 c. chopped nuts
1/2 c. raisins

Mix together the sugars and oil. Add eggs and pumpkin; mix well. Sift dry ingredients together and add to pumpkin mixture. Stir in nuts and raisins. Pour batter into a well-greased and floured 2-pound metal coffee can. Place in slow cooker and cover top of can with 6 to 8 paper towels to absorb condensation. Cover and cook on high setting for 2-1/2 to 3-1/2 hours. Cake is done when toothpick inserted in center comes out clean. Serves 8.

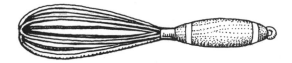

Peach Cobbler

Sue Learned
Wilton, CA

Pour cream over top for an old-fashioned delight.

3/4 c. biscuit baking mix	3/4 c. evaporated milk
1/3 c. sugar	2 t. butter, melted
1/2 c. brown sugar, packed	3 peaches, pitted and mashed
2 eggs, beaten	3/4 t. cinnamon
2 t. vanilla extract	Optional: vanilla ice cream

In a large bowl, combine baking mix and sugars. Add eggs and vanilla; stir. Pour in evaporated milk and butter; stir. Add peaches and cinnamon; mix well. Pour into a lightly greased slow cooker. Cover and cook on low setting for 6 to 8 hours, or on high setting for 3 to 4 hours. Serve warm, topped with ice cream if desired. Makes 6 servings.

Serve ice cream-topped desserts to a party crowd, the quick & easy way! Scoop ice cream ahead of time and freeze in paper muffin liners.

Apple Brown Betty

Amy Crowe-Galloway
Pontotoc, MS

With a slow cooker, it's so easy to make this yummy old-fashioned favorite! 3 lbs. cooking apples, cored, peeled and cut into eighths

10 slices bread, cubed
1/2 t. cinnamon
1/4 t. nutmeg
1/8 t. salt

3/4 c. brown sugar, packed
1/2 c. butter, melted
Garnish: whipped topping

Place apples in a slow cooker. Combine remaining ingredients except topping; toss together and sprinkle over apples. Cover and cook on low setting 2 to 4 hours. Garnish with whipped topping. Makes 6 to 8 servings.

Stock up during berry-picking season for delicious desserts! Lay unwashed berries on baking sheets and freeze, then pack into bags for the freezer. When you're ready to use them, rinse berries in a colander. They'll thaw quickly.

Indian Pudding

Joanne Mello
North Dartmouth, MA

*Every Thanksgiving, I make this traditional New England dessert
that's reminiscent of the first Thanksgiving.*

3 c. milk
1/2 c. cornmeal
1/2 t. salt
3 eggs, beaten
1/4 c. light brown sugar, packed
1/3 c. molasses

2 T. butter, diced
1/2 t. cinnamon
1/2 t. ground ginger
1/4 t. allspice
Garnish: vanilla ice cream

Lightly grease slow cooker; preheat on high setting for 20 minutes.
Bring milk, cornmeal and salt to a boil in a saucepan. Boil, stirring
constantly, for 5 minutes. Reduce heat; cover and simmer for
10 minutes. Combine remaining ingredients except ice cream in a
large bowl; gradually beat in hot milk mixture and whisk until smooth.
Pour into slow cooker; cover and cook on low setting for 6 to 8 hours,
or on high setting for 2 to 3 hours. Serve warm, topped with ice
cream. Makes 4 servings.

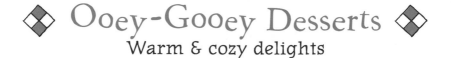

◆ Ooey-Gooey Desserts ◆
Warm & cozy delights

Lemon-Poppy Seed Cake

Rogene Rogers
Bemidji, MN

An upside-down cake that makes its own custard-like topping...yum!

15.8-oz. lemon-poppy seed
    bread mix
1 egg, beaten
8-oz. container sour cream

1-1/4 c. water, divided
1 T. butter
1/2 c. sugar
1/4 c. lemon juice

Combine bread mix, egg, sour cream and 1/2 cup water in a mixing bowl. Stir until well moistened; spread in a lightly greased slow cooker. Combine remaining water, butter, sugar and lemon juice in a small saucepan; bring to a boil. Pour boiling mixture over batter in slow cooker; cover and cook on high setting for 2 to 2-1/2 hours. Edges will be golden. Turn off slow cooker; let cake cool in slow cooker for about 30 minutes with lid ajar. When cool enough to handle, hold a large plate over top of slow cooker and invert to turn out cake. Serves 10 to 12.

Use corks to stamp polka dots on flowerpots with craft paint, then plant with bright-colored flowers...fun table decorations for a dessert party!

Creamy Rice Pudding

Shelley Sparks
Amarillo, TX

A tummy-warming treat.

1 pt. half-and-half
3 eggs
2/3 c. sugar
2 t. vanilla extract

1-1/2 c. cooked rice
3/4 c. raisins
1/2 t. nutmeg
1/2 t. cinnamon

In a mixing bowl, beat half-and-half, eggs, sugar and vanilla with an electric mixer on medium speed. Stir in rice and raisins. Pour into a greased slow cooker; sprinkle with nutmeg and cinnamon. Cover and cook on high setting for 30 minutes; stir well. Cover; reduce setting to low and cook for 2 to 3 hours. Makes 8 to 10 servings.

Tuck fresh-cut blue cornflowers into a vintage
milk glass pitcher...how sweet.

Ooey-Gooey Desserts
Warm & cozy delights

Steamed Cranberry Pudding

Janet Girouard
Jaffrey, NH

This is a favorite of my family at Christmas…I predict it will become one of your favorites too!

2 T. butter, softened
2 T. sugar
1-1/3 c. all-purpose flour
1 t. baking powder
1 t. baking soda

1/2 t. salt
2 c. cranberries, halved
1/2 c. molasses
1/3 c. hot water

Butter a one-pound metal coffee can or pudding mold that will fit into your slow cooker; sprinkle with sugar and set aside. Combine flour, baking powder, baking soda and salt in a mixing bowl; stir in berries. Add molasses and hot water; mix well and pour into prepared can or mold. Place 2 paper towels on top of can to absorb condensation; cover tightly with aluminum foil. Set can in slow cooker; pour about 2 inches of water around can. Cover and cook on high setting for 5 to 6 hours. Let cool 10 minutes; turn pudding out of can. Slice and serve with Butter Sauce. Makes 8 servings.

Butter Sauce:

1/2 c. butter, sliced
1/2 c. light cream

1 c. sugar
1 t. vanilla extract

In a medium saucepan, bring all ingredients to a boil; reduce heat and cook for 4 minutes. Serve warm.

Teach your slow cooker some new tricks!

Savory Chicken Broth

In a large slow cooker, combine 4 pounds chicken thighs, 2 onions, 2 carrots and 2 stalks celery, coarsely chopped, and 8 peppercorns. Add 8 cups cold water; cover and cook on high setting for one hour. Turn to low setting; cook for 6 to 10 hours. Cool for one hour. Strain broth into a bowl, reserving cooked chicken for another use. Refrigerate broth; skim fat from surface. Refrigerate up to 3 days or freeze up to 3 months. Makes about 8 cups.

Freshly Baked Bread

Rub a one-pound loaf of frozen bread dough generously with oil. Place in a greased loaf pan or round cake pan. Place pan in a large slow cooker; cover and cook on low setting for 2 to 3 hours, until dough is thawed and beginning to rise. Turn setting to high; cover and cook an additional 2 to 3 hours, until loaf is golden and sounds hollow when tapped. Makes one loaf.

Sunny Apricot Preserves

Finely chop one pound dried apricots; combine with 3-1/2 cups water and 1-3/4 cups sugar in a medium slow cooker. Cover and cook on high setting for 2-1/2 hours, stirring twice. Turn to low setting; uncover and cook an additional 2 hours, until thickened, stirring occasionally. Cool; spoon into sterile glass or plastic containers. Keep refrigerated up to 3 weeks. Makes 4 to 5 cups.

Curried Fruit Chutney

Chop one onion and five, 7-ounce packages of dried fruit: two of dried mixed fruit, two of dried apricots and one of dried plums. Combine in a slow cooker with 1/2 cup raisins, 2 cups water, 1-1/2 cups cider vinegar, 3/4 cup sugar, 2 teaspoons curry powder, 1/4 teaspoon salt, 1/4 teaspoon ground ginger and 1/8 teaspoon cayenne pepper. Cover and cook on low setting for 4 to 5 hours, until fruit is tender. Cool; spoon into sterile glass or plastic containers. Keep refrigerated up to 3 weeks or frozen up to 3 months. Makes about 6 cups.

Spicy Hot Roast Nuts

Place 2 cups raw cashews, pecans or almonds in a medium slow cooker. Mix in one teaspoon chili powder, 1/2 teaspoon cayenne powder and 1/4 teaspoon cinnamon. Cover and cook on high setting for 1-1/2 hours, stirring every 15 to 30 minutes, until nuts are toasted. Combine one tablespoon olive oil and 2 teaspoon salt; stir into nuts. Store in an airtight container. Makes 2 cups.

Baked Potatoes

Pierce 6 to 8 baking potatoes several times with a fork. Rub softened butter generously over potatoes and arrange in a large slow cooker. Cover and cook on low setting for 6 to 9 hours, or on high setting for 3 to 5 hours, until tender. Makes 6 to 8.

Caramelized Onions

Place 3 pounds sliced sweet onions, 1/2 cup diced butter and one teaspoon salt in a slow cooker. Cover and cook on low setting for 8 to 10 hours, until soft and golden. Use immediately or refrigerate up to 3 days. Makes about 3 cups.

❖INDEX❖

❖INDEX❖

❖INDEX❖

Find Gooseberry Patch
wherever you are!

www.gooseberrypatch.com

Email   Blog   YouTube

Call us toll-free at 1·800·854·6673

simmering soups • fix & go

piping hot

fork-tender roasts

hearty fare

yummy aromas

comfort food

get it!   come & get it!   tummy-warming

U.S. to Metric Recipe Equivalents

Volume Measurements

1/4 teaspoon	1 mL
1/2 teaspoon	2 mL
1 teaspoon	5 mL
1 tablespoon = 3 teaspoons	15 mL
2 tablespoons = 1 fluid ounce	30 mL
1/4 cup	60 mL
1/3 cup	75 mL
1/2 cup = 4 fluid ounces	125 mL
1 cup = 8 fluid ounces	250 mL
2 cups = 1 pint =16 fluid ounces	500 mL
4 cups = 1 quart	1 L

Weights

1 ounce	30 g
4 ounces	120 g
8 ounces	225 g
16 ounces = 1 pound	450 g

Oven Temperatures

300° F	150° C
325° F	160° C
350° F	180° C
375° F	190° C
400° F	200° C
450° F	230° C

Baking Pan Sizes

Square		Loaf	
8x8x2 inches	2 L = 20x20x5 cm	9x5x3 inches	2 L = 23x13x7 cm
9x9x2 inches	2.5 L = 23x23x5 cm	Round	
Rectangular		8x1-1/2 inches	1.2 L = 20x4 cm
13x9x2 inches	3.5 L = 33x23x5 cm	9x1-1/2 inches	1.5 L = 23x4 cm